Understanding the People and Performance Link: Unlocking the black box

John Purcell

Nick Kinnie

Sue Hutchinson

Bruce Rayton

Juani Swart

Work and Employment Research Centre,

School of Management, University of Bath

First published 2003
Reprinted 2003, 2004, 2005, 2006, 2007, 2008, 2009

Cover design by Curve
Designed and typeset by Beacon GDT
Printed in Great Britain by Short Run Press

British Library Cataloguing in Publication Data
A catalogue record for this book is available from the British Library

ISBN 0 85292 987 0
ISBN-13 978 0 85292 987 2

Chartered Institute of Personnel and Development,
151 The Broadway, London SW19 1JQ

Tel: 020 8612 6200
Website: www.cipd.co.uk

Incorporated by Royal Charter. Registered charity no. 1079797.

Understanding the People and Performance Link: Unlocking the black box

John Purcell

Nick Kinnie

Sue Hutchinson

Bruce Rayton

Juani Swart

The Chartered Institute of Personnel and Development is the leading publisher of books and reports for personnel and training professionals, students, and all those concerned with the effective management and development of people at work. For full details of all our titles, please contact the Publishing Department:

Tel: 020 8612 6204

E-mail: publish@cipd.co.uk

To view and purchase the full range of CIPD publications:
www.cipd.co.uk/bookstore

Contents

Acknowledgements

We are deeply indebted to the senior HR managers and executives in the 12 organisations concerned in this research, and listed in Chapter 1, for their time, patience and enthusiasm in co-operating in this research project. Our thanks also extends to the middle managers and the employee representatives we interviewed and the many employees who took part by answering complex questions not just once, but twice.

Dr Kim Hoque helped with the data collection and early interpretation before he moved on to Nottingham Business School. A number of doctoral students helped with the interviews when the core team were stretched. Cathy Aubin, the WERC Secretary, managed the administration, data entry and report editing superbly. We thank them all.

List of tables and figures

Tables

Figures

Foreword

This report represents the culmination of six years of study for the Chartered Institute of Personnel and Development. In 1997 the Institute recognised that this issue of the impact that people management practice could make on overall business performance was critical to the future development of our profession. However, although a plethora of evidence already existed at that time demonstrating that best practice in people management co-existed with better business results, it was open to criticism from a number of sources.

The critics argued that because the majority of studies at that time had been carried out in manufacturing where issues such as productivity were easier to manage, the results would not be replicated in the service sector. They further argued that high-performing companies could afford to invest in better people management and that therefore people management practice did not necessarily cause better bottom-line results.

As a result the CIPD developed a programme of work which focused on three specific aims:

◻ to improve the evidence linking people management to business performance or organisational competitiveness

◻ to provide accessible information on which managers can act through effective choices and decisions

◻ to improve understanding of why and how people management practices influence business performance.

A central plank of our research programme has therefore been to look at this issue of causality. Previous research carried out for the CIPD led by

Professor David Guest of King's College, University of London, addressed much of this criticism and strengthened the argument that better people management causes better business performance rather than simply co-exists with it. The aim of this later research commissioned from the team at Bath University led by Professor John Purcell was to look inside the black box to try to understand the relationship between people management and performance.

The results, which John and his team review in this report, are already proving extremely valuable and highly insightful to the people management profession. This work is probably the most in-depth study of its kind to date and has collected a wealth of attitudinal data from a cross-section of employees in each of the 12 companies studied. It has provided an immense pool of information on which to draw to support the conclusions. It has surpassed our original aims and clearly demonstrates the central role of people management in developing and sustaining a high performing organisation.

In addition the team have produced a detailed model of the people and performance relationship and the cause and effect of practice.

The CIPD is confident that this work has a major role to play in shaping and developing the contribution of the people management profession to business. This report is therefore only the start of a dissemination process that is not just about providing knowledge but also about supporting the implementation of the results of this research into practice.

Angela Baron

Adviser, Organisation and Resourcing
Chartered Institute of Personnel and Development

Executive summary

The aim of this study was to examine the impact of people management on organisational performance. Many previous studies have examined the link between HR practices and policies and shown there to be a positive relationship, but none has explained the nature of this connection – in other words, how and why HR practices impact on performance.

This is commonly referred to as the 'black box' problem, and the main purpose of our study was to unlock the 'black box' to show the way in which HR practices – or what the CIPD terms 'people management', meaning all aspects of how people are managed – impact on performance.

The study was conducted within a framework which claims that performance is a function of Ability + Motivation + Opportunity (referred to as AMO). Essentially this means that people perform well when, firstly, they are able to do so because they possess the necessary knowledge and skills; when, secondly, they have the motivation to do so, and do it well; and when, thirdly, they are given the opportunity to deploy their skills both in the job, and more broadly in contributing to their work groups and organisational success.

A range of HR policies and practices are required to turn this into action. We identified 11 in our model, covering recruitment and selection, training and development, career opportunity, communications, involvement in decision-making, teamworking, appraisal, pay, job security, job challenge/job autonomy and work–life balance. These performance-related HR policies encourage people to exercise a degree of choice on how and how well they do their job. In other words, they help induce discretionary behaviour which makes people work better and improve performance. This happens because the HR policies and practices

develop positive employee attitudes or feelings of satisfaction, commitment and motivation.

This report presents the findings of this study which centred on 12 organisations from a wide range of sectors, all of which were known for their quality of human resource management or were actively seeking to improve the link between people management and performance. In each case we focused on a unit of analysis, an identifiable area of the business, where we conducted extensive interviewing with front-line employees – in other words, those at the receiving end of the HR policies and practices. This data was gathered twice over a two-and-a-half-year period in order for us to track changes in attitudes. It was examined alongside other data from interviews with senior and line managers, performance measures and additional information on HR policies for the unit of analysis.

One of the keys to the HR–performance link is the existence of a 'Big Idea', a clear mission underpinned by values and a culture expressing what the organisation stands for and is trying to achieve. In Jaguar, for example, the Big Idea is quality; in Nationwide it is 'mutuality'. In our case studies the existence of the Big Idea was strongly linked to employee commitment.

Organisations with a Big Idea displayed five common characteristics – the Idea was embedded, connected, enduring, collective and 'measured and managed'. The Big Idea therefore means more than just having a formal mission statement. It means that the values are spread throughout the organisation so that they are embedded in policies and practices. These values interconnect the relationships with customers (both internal and external), culture and behaviour, and provide the basis upon which employees should be managed.

This was particularly evident in customer-facing organisations in our study. The values were also enduring or long-lasting even during the difficult times, and provided a stable basis on which policies could be built and changed. The Big Idea was also a collective endeavour or a sort of glue binding people and processes together in one common goal. Finally, the Idea could be managed and measured, often through a balanced-scorecard type of approach which provided not just the means of measuring performance but also a way of integrating different functional areas of the business, both horizontally and vertically.

Fairly early on in our research it became evident that front line management or leadership has a crucial role to play in terms of implementing and enacting HR policies, practices and values. In other words, these managers 'bring policies to life'. It is not enough just to have performance-enhancing HR policies and practices – what also matters is the way they are implemented. Managers have discretion in the way they practise good people management in the sense of, for example, communicating, solving problems, listening to employee suggestions, providing coaching and guidance, treating employees fairly, and showing respect.

Employees in turn are more likely to go 'beyond contract' or that 'extra mile' for the organisation if managers behave in ways that stimulate and encourage positive attitudes. Employee discretion is therefore affected by the way in which managers exercise their own discretion.

Some of the organisations in the study made significant attempts to improve line management behaviour during the course of the research, and this was clearly reflected in improved employee attitudes and performance.

Some HR policies and practices were shown to be particularly important in terms of influencing employee outcomes like commitment, job satisfaction and motivation. These were those concerned with career opportunities, job influence, job challenge, training, performance appraisal, teamworking, involvement in decision-making, work–life balance, and having managers who are good at leadership and who show respect.

In addition, however, we found that employee dissatisfaction with existing policies had a greater impact in terms of lowering commitment than did the absence of given policies. The implication of this is that getting existing policies to work better will be more likely to pay dividends in terms of increasing employee commitment than developing new policies. This re-emphasises the crucial role that line managers have to play in implementing policies and practices.

There were clear differences between occupational groups in the way employees responded to various policies and practices. For team leaders and junior managers, their relationship with their boss, the openness of the organisation (in terms of allowing them to discuss issues of concern to them), career opportunities, and training were the most important issues. For professionals (those who would normally require some kind of externally certified education or training, such as accountants and nurses), job challenge, management leadership, linking pay to performance, work–life balance and the climate of manager–employee relations were key factors. Employees, however, were particularly concerned to have some influence over their job, job challenge, job security, career opportunities, and a sense of involvement.

In some organisations it was possible to demonstrate a clear association between people management and performance. However, as with previous research, difficulties in obtaining performance data limited our ability to conduct the kinds of analysis we would have liked. In some organisations, for example, the relevant data for the unit of analysis was simply not available. In others there was too much data. It was also difficult to isolate the impact of policies and practices from other factors, such as technology or market fluctuations.

Nevertheless, there was strong evidence in a number of organisations that, when effectively managed, some HR policies and practices showed positive associations with performance. In one organisation we also found that some poorly managed HR policies and practices had negative outcomes.

Undoubtedly, however, the most successful organisations were those that could sustain their performance over the long term and demonstrate a robust association between people management and performance. This meant that the HR policies and practices 'fitted' with business strategy, while at the same time were flexible enough to help adapt to new environments. In these circumstances organisations were able to sustain performance even when external competitive pressures placed the link between people management and performance under strain.

The research suggests a number of policy implications. Organisations seeking to optimise the contribution that people management can make must develop policies and practices that meet the needs of individuals and create 'a great place to work'. However, this does not just mean copying 'best practice'. Organisations must create and transmit values and culture which are unique to themselves, which bind the organisation together,

and which can be measured and managed. HR management must not be a stand-alone function but be fully integrated into the management process – its contribution must be valued.

Attention should also focus on those policies and practices that have been shown to be particularly important in influencing employee attitudes and creating positive discretionary behaviour. These include those directed at careers, training, job design, and involve communication, appraisal and work–life balance. Attention must focus on front line leadership – those who are responsible for implementing the policies and practices. They need training and support, not just in terms of providing the right policy tools to do the job well, but from above – from the middle and upper management tier that supports them.

Finally, internal company measures and data are highly important as a means to identify problems, monitor progress and link all aspects of the business – including people management policies and practices – with values and the Big Idea.

1 | How can we explain the connection between people management and performance?

Background

There is widespread evidence that the way a firm manages its employees influences organisational performance. It is surprisingly difficult, however, to find out how this takes place. It is often easier to see what happens when things go wrong – when problems of rising labour turnover, absenteeism and conflict reflect poor human resource management (HRM) and impact negatively on organisational performance.

In high-performing firms, in contrast, the sources of competitiveness often remain hidden from view and thus are difficult to analyse. Indeed, this is one of their strengths. High-performing firms are hard to copy, and it is this rare ability to combine able people and complex work and social processes which helps sustain good performance beyond the immediate and short term.

This resource advantage has been the subject of numerous studies.

- Some look at leadership.

- Others survey the way technology is deployed.

- Functional specialists focus on aspects of their own area such as marketing, operations, finance and so on.

- But in recent years it is the management of people which has attracted the most attention.

This attention is not just from HRM specialists but also from experts in business strategy. One good reason for this is because the physical, tangible resources a firm can deploy are harder to protect, easier to copy, and depreciate faster than previously. Intangible assets such as culture, skill and competence, motivation and social interaction between people, teams and business units, are increasingly seen as key sources of strength in those firms that can combine people and processes together. These are generally referred to as 'human capital advantage' and 'organisational process advantage' (Boxall and Purcell, 2003: 85–86).

In short (ibid):
Human resource advantage can be traced to better people employed in organisations with better processes.

This 'human resource advantage' is easier to assert than study, and much easier to describe than prove. In the decade from the early/mid-1990s our understanding has improved hugely, yet problems remain.

There have, in the main, been two approaches to try to tackle the question of the extent to which people management impacts on organisational performance.

Data sets

One approach relies on the generation of large data sets covering as many organisations as possible across the economy, allowing for patterns to be observed between profit (or market value) per employee and a measure of HRM sophistication. This measure is usually a count of the number of named HR policies or practices the firm uses, sometimes adjusted to the proportion of

> ' **In the decade from the early/mid-1990s our understanding has improved hugely, yet problems remain.**'

employees covered or the extent of use. It relies on postal questionnaires mostly filled in by one respondent.

Impressive results showing a clear association between the number of HR practices and profit or market value are revealed in this approach, especially in the manufacturing sector where these studies predominated. The fact that Guest's results in the UK (2001) are similar to earlier work in the USA by Huselid (1995) adds to the confidence that can be placed in this approach.

Two problems remain, however.

First, it is impossible to know for certain about the direction of causation. Although it is nice to believe that more HR practices leads to higher economic return, it is just as possible to argue that it is successful firms that can afford more extensive (and expensive) HRM practices. However, even if this reverse causality were true, the fact is that successful firms do invest heavily in HRM. The presumption is that they do this in order to help sustain performance by replication and adaptation.

This issue of sustainability is one we return to later in this report.

The second limitation is that we do not know why or how HR policies translate into performance. This is known as the 'black box' problem. We can look at inputs in terms of policies and practices and adjust for various circumstances or contingencies, and we can look at outputs like profit per person employed, but the actual links or levers (better thought of as processes) that connect inputs and outputs are hidden from view.

It was this 'black box problem' which led the CIPD to commission the research reported here.

Sector-specific comparisons

The other main type of research approach looking for the interconnection between people and performance is sector-specific, by which firms in one industry are compared while common factors in the sector such as technology and market conditions are taken out of the analysis.

This allows for much closer connection between business strategy and HRM strategy to be observed, and for more meaningful performance links to be established. Rates of return on capital, or sales and thus profits per employee, vary widely between sectors. But within this 'industry effect' there are high performers and laggards, pointing to the crucial importance of strategic choice in the past and the present and to help shape the future. These choices include people management.

A growing number of sector studies have been published in recent years using a variety of performance measures better suited to the particular sector. These range from mortality rates in hospitals (West *et al*, 2002) to sales performance in call centres (Batt and Moynihan, 2002), added value in aerospace (Thompson, 2000), costs in the clothing or apparel industry (Berg *et al*, 1996) and scrap rates in steel minimills (Arthur, 1992, 1994).

Sector studies allow for more refinement in the choice of appropriate performance outcome measures. To take a global measure of profit or market value is to use a single measure that is susceptible to a wide variety of influences, only one of which is the management of people – and this may well be a long way upstream in the value chain before it turns into profit.

Understanding the People and Performance Link: Unlocking the black box | **3**

How can we explain the connection between people management and performance?

> ' ... we do not know why or how HR policies
> translate into performance. This is known as the
> "black box" problem.'

Sector studies get closer but they, too, rarely have the means to get inside the black box since most rely on questionnaires sent to single respondents in each firm, collecting only management views. They are often able to be more precise about which HR practices are particularly influential, drawing attention to factors like job design, skill acquisition, teamworking, appraisal or performance management generally. This still leaves the question open on how these policies translate into performance.

Making comparisons between firms in a sector is useful, but one-off, snapshot surveys taken at one point in time are limited, since it is impossible to trace dynamic interrelationships between people management and performance. Thompson's longitudinal study in Aerospace (2000) has usefully done this, but few others have been able to.

Macro-HR

These two approaches to research on the connection between people management and performance coincide with the ongoing debate about the design of HR systems or the HR architecture of the firm (sometimes called 'macro-HR'). Is there a universal prescription of best practice that should be applied to all organisations if only top management, and the stock market, recognised its importance?

Such a 'best practice' approach is easy to understand, and by advocating a win–win approach is appealing. But is it too simple, and why do so few organisations adopt it?

An alternative is to ask how HR architecture could be modelled more closely to fit with the prevailing business strategy and position in the firm's life-cycle from emergent, small, new firms to mature larger ones, and those in decline. This 'best fit'

approach is evident in sector studies where the connection between strategy and HR can be studied in some depth.

A good example of this is Arthur's study of steel minimills (1992, 1994) in the USA in which those mills seeking to achieve cost leadership by having the lowest production costs and thus lowest prices by reducing product variety were observed almost universally to adopt a cost-minimisation command-and-control type of HR. Here jobs are designed to minimise the need for training, wages are low, and non-productive time as taken up by problem-solving teams is minimised.

In contrast, two-thirds of steel minimills going for product and quality differentiation, meeting customer needs through product variety, adopted a high-commitment management (HCM) or high-performance work system (HPWS) HR system, to use the American term. This is where a 'bundle' of HR practices including emphasis on training, employee problem-solving, teamworking, higher pay, a higher proportion of skilled employees and supervisors with attempts to create a work community (seen in social events) are used to enhance performance in quality and delivery times.

This distinction between best practice and best fit is not the whole story, however. Although best fit is more subtle and more convincing, it suffers from a number of drawbacks.

◘ First, it is impossible to isolate all of the influences (or contingencies) that inform, and constrain, choice in HR.

◘ Second, even if it were possible to model every influence – from business strategy to the external environment in the labour market, including legislation – this fit would be static.

> ' ... the need is not just to find the right fit now but to have the flexibility to meet future challenges.'

Since there is growing uncertainty in markets from how competitors change through development in technologies, new regulations introduced, and the economic cycle, the need is not just to find the right fit now but to have the flexibility to meet future challenges.

Pat Wright and Scott Snell (1998) from Cornell University in the USA argue this powerfully. They suggest that the need is to achieve fit with existing competitive strategy while simultaneously achieving flexibility in a range of skills and behaviours that may be needed to cope with different competitive scenarios in the future. Thus (Boxall and Purcell, 2003: 56) argue that:

Aiming to meet current competitive needs in a cost-effective way is important, but so too are goals for supporting organisational flexibility over time … And throughout all of this, there is a need to motivate employees by meeting their goals as far as possible … and complying with labour laws and social norms for employing labour.

These tensions between 'now' and 'the future' and between focusing on competitive strategy and meeting employee needs mean that a simple definition of performance as a single measure like 'profit' or 'shareholder values' is never sufficient. Past performance in changing circumstances is an unreliable guide to future success. Classic accountancy measures are trailing or lagged indicators. Leading indicators like customer loyalty or employee commitment are increasingly used to refine performance measures.

These leading indicators suggest that the sources of sustained competitive advantage are more often found within the organisation than externally in the competitive environment.

Rather than look for a given number of good or appropriate HR policies and practices and link these to performance, the need in this approach – in which resource strength is important for medium- and long-term success – is to ask what happens when these policies and practices are implemented. That is the focus on processes. Can we identify best processes that help to create and sustain performance?

This was the challenge set us by the CIPD. Could we open the black box to show the way in which HR practices – or what the CIPD helpfully called 'people management', meaning all aspects of how people are managed – impact on performance?

This report gives a summary of the results of a large and complex study.

In this chapter we briefly explain how we conducted the research in 12 case-study organisations. This is important, since there is often a trade-off between breadth and depth in research design which influences the generalisability of the results compared with the richness of findings in single cases.

First, however, we need to show and explain the central explanatory model built to provide the basis for our work. This 'theory section' is again very important since, if correct, it holds the basis for understanding how people management impacts on performance. Collecting the evidence and interpreting the results, in outline, is what makes up the rest of this report.

The Bath People and Performance model

If we can show a link between HR practices and measures of performance outcomes, we must have certain propositions of why this link exists.

Understanding the People and Performance Link: Unlocking the black box | **5**

How can we explain the connection between people management and performance?

> ' **The fundamental model asserts that performance is a function of Ability + Motivation + Opportunity (this is known as AMO).**'

This takes us back to the fundamental purpose of HRM. Here we can assert that for people to perform better, beyond the minimal requirements, they must:

- ☐ have the ability to do so because they possess the necessary knowledge and skills, including how to work with other people

- ☐ be motivated to do the work, and do it well

- ☐ be given the opportunity to deploy their skills both in the job and more broadly contributing to work-group and organisational success.

The fundamental model (Boxall and Purcell, 2003: 20) asserts that performance is a function of Ability + Motivation + Opportunity (this is known as AMO). The question is what sort of policies and practices are required for AMO to be turned into action.

Some obvious first thoughts draw attention to recruitment, selection and training linked to ability; rewards (a complex area) for motivation; and involvement in the job and beyond it for opportunity. But this listing of policies is not enough and gets more complex once we recognise that a whole variety of different policies can be used under these generic headings and that people vary in their response to policy initiatives.

This response to AMO policies is the key to the performance-enhancing model. In most jobs, bar the most routine and simple repetitive tasks, people have discretion or some degree of choice on how, and how well, they are to do the job.

Discretionary behaviour means making the sort of choices that often define a job, such as the way the job is done – the speed, care, innovation and

style of job delivery. This behaviour is at the heart of the employment relationship, because it is hard for the employer to define and then monitor and control the amount of effort, innovation and productive behaviour required. The most obvious example here is front-line service work dealing with customers either face to face or over the telephone. It concerns the sort of everyday behaviour that the employer wants but has to rely on the employee to deliver. It may involve emotional labour (smiling down the phone), using knowledge to solve a problem or to suggest an alternative to the customer, or it may be internal to the work of the organisation, such as co-operating with team members, helping probationers learn shortcuts or sharing new ideas on work processes. One way or the other, the employee chooses how conscientiously to undertake the job.

Most jobs are built up of many tasks, so the level of complexity can be surprisingly high, even for seemingly routine ones. The choice of how, and how well, to do things is not necessarily made deliberately: it can be unconscious – just part of the way people behave in their organisation. But discretionary behaviour can certainly be withdrawn, often in the sense of adopting an uncaring attitude. This may be a reciprocal response to a belief that 'the firm no longer cares about me, my future or my opinions'.

Ultimately, whatever the incentives or sanctions the firm tries to use, it lies with the employee to 'give' discretionary behaviour and to withdraw it. Although this is described in terms of the action of an individual (we all have bad days), it is the collective withdrawal of discretionary behaviour that is so damaging. Our own experience tells us that there are times when morale is low, or the 'buzz' has gone, or everyone just wants to go home as soon as possible.

> ' ... effective firms have a level of sophistication in their approach to people management which helps induce discretionary behaviour and above-average performance.'

The obvious proverb here is that 'You can take a horse to water but you cannot make it drink.' The important question then is what persuades, induces or encourages people to utilise their discretion in improving job performance?

■ The assumption in A (Ability) is that people will want to apply for jobs in an organisation (recruitment), have their attributes recognised (selection) and be willing to learn new skills and behaviours (training and development).

■ In M (Motivation) the assumption is that people can be motivated to use their ability in a productive manner because they will respond to various extrinsic and intrinsic rewards and stimuli.

■ In O (Opportunity) the assumption is that people will provide good customer service, or high-quality work beyond the satisfactory level, and will wish to engage in problem-solving or wider involvement schemes, given the opportunities to do so. They need the opportunity both to use or practise their skills and to contribute to collective efforts at the team, section and organisation level. In other words, to have the opportunity to participate in these efforts both in doing their job and in the organisation.

Employers thus need to have some basic AMO policies in order to meet minimum industry standards for survival, but effective firms have a level of sophistication in their approach to people management which helps induce discretionary behaviour and above-average performance.

This focus on discretionary behaviour is now central to some contemporary research in people and performance, such as the work of Appelbaum and her colleagues in manufacturing in the USA

(2000) and Wright and Gardiner in their study of a single customer service firm (2003), and to the research we have been doing and report here.

Once we accept the connection between discretionary behaviour and performance, the next question is what causes or helps trigger this discretionary behaviour?

We have asserted a link between a broad range of AMO policies and the need for these to induce, or encourage discretion through selecting, training, motivating and involving people, especially where the job performed depends on what some economists call 'consummate co-operation'. Discretionary behaviour is hard to study despite its common sense appeal.

We know from a variety of studies in what is called 'organisational citizenship behaviour' (OCB) that 'going the extra mile' (whether it be in customer service, ensuring quality, engaging in problem-solving, or helping others) is strongly linked to people's perceptions of their employer, how satisfying they find their job, and how strongly they feel motivated to undertake it (Coyle-Shapiro *et al*, 2000, and forthcoming). So if enough people feel committed to the organisation that employs them to the extent that they feel proud to tell people who they work for and want to stay working for the firm for the foreseeable future (what is called affective commitment), they are more likely to engage in discretionary behaviour to help the firm be successful. This usually applies too when they feel motivated and when the job gives them high levels of satisfaction.

For some employees all three of these attributes (commitment, motivation and satisfaction) are interconnected. For others it may be just one that is the link with discretionary behaviour. We look at this in the next chapter.

Understanding the People and Performance Link: Unlocking the black box | 7

How can we explain the connection between people management and performance?

One of the prime functions of AMO policies is thus the way they help develop attitudes or feelings of satisfaction, commitment and motivation in most employees since these translate into discretionary behaviour, provided the job allows for it. This is why there is so much interest in organisational commitment and motivation and in associated concepts like the psychological contract and organisational citizenship behaviour. The link is shown in the model displayed as Figure 1.

Figure 1 | The People and Performance model

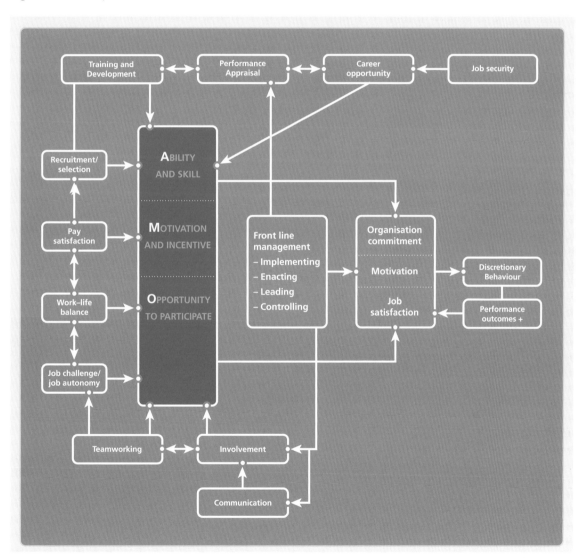

' ... nearly all HR policies are applied through and by line managers. It is these managers who bring policies to life.'

In the model, AMO in the bold purple box feed directly into the three elements of organisational commitment, motivation and job satisfaction. This is the central assertion. There are three other important dimensions.

First, on the outside ring 11 policy or practice areas in HRM are identified to feed into and give practical meaning to AMO, and are themselves interrelated one with another. They are:

- careful/sophisticated recruitment and selection

- training and learning/development

- an emphasis on providing career opportunities

- information-sharing and extensive two-way communication

- involvement in decision-making

- teamworking

- appraising each individual's performance and development

- pay satisfaction

- job security

- job challenge/job autonomy

- work–life balance.

The 11 practices shown here were identified from previous research as likely to be of importance. This is a controversial area: different researchers have presented different lists of policies, especially those concerned with producing one 'best practice' model.

In 1994 Pfeffer produced a list of 16 practices 'for competitive advantage through people'. By 1998 this had been reduced to seven practices for 'building profits by putting people first'. For our research we tested some 18 practice areas and identified the 11 shown in the model as being the most universal and the most likely to be of importance.

The second crucial feature of the People and Performance model is the central box – front-line management – which is between AMO and the commitment, motivation and satisfaction box. This draws attention to the fact that nearly all HR policies are applied through and by line managers. It is these managers who bring policies to life.

In a broader sense, organisational culture and values are often experienced by workers through the behaviour of front-line managers in the way these managers show respect, exhibit trust, respond to suggestions, give directions, and behave. We call this front-line leadership since in effect front-line managers have a crucial role in translating policies and practices, and wider cultures and values, into actions. Much of what they do in this area – especially in the way they do it – is also discretionary. We discuss this in Chapter 3.

Finally, the arrow going back from performance outcomes to attitudes in the bottom right-hand end of the model draws attention to the feedback effect. People generally like working for successful organisations and the experience of success, especially if shared, feeds back to help reinforce attitudes. This also sometimes means that people attribute success to policies even where there may be no actual connection.

> ' **The research design was both qualitative and quantitative … , and focused on 12 organisations from a wide range of sectors … .'**

As Wright and Gardener (2000) say, it makes life difficult for researchers who endeavour to test the link. The problem of attribution can operate in reverse when performance declines. Such 'halo' and 'horn' effects can be self-fulfilling, but 'halos' can turn into 'horns' when something breaches trust between employees and managers or the firm more broadly, such as unfairness or inequities in decision-making or application. This is especially likely to happen when traumatic change overtakes an organisation, like major redundancies, re-organisation or merger.

In summary, our propositions are:

- Performance-related HR practices work only if they positively induce discretionary behaviour once basic staffing requirements have been met.

- Discretionary behaviour is more likely to occur when enough individuals have commitment to their organisation and/or when they feel motivated to act in such a way and/or when they gain high levels of job satisfaction.

- Commitment, motivation and job satisfaction, either together or separately, are greater when people positively experience the application of HR policies concerned with creating an able workforce, motivating valued behaviours and providing opportunities to participate.

- This positive experience is better if the wide range of HR policies necessary for AMO are in place and are mutually reinforcing.

- The way policies and practices are implemented by front-line managers and the way top-level espoused values and organisational cultures are enacted by them enhances or weakens the effect of HR policies in triggering discretionary behaviour by influencing attitudes.

- The experience of success seen in performance outcomes helps to reinforce positive attitudes.

The research design

These detailed propositions and more generally our interest in unlocking the 'black box' shaped our research design. Research commenced in September 1999 and spanned just over two-and-a-half years.

The research design was both qualitative and quantitative in nature, and focused on 12 organisations from a wide range of sectors including manufacturing, retail, finance, professional services, IT and the NHS. These organisations were either known for their quality of human resource management or were actively seeking to improve the link between people management and performance.

In each case we chose a unit of analysis to be the focus of our research, as outlined in Table 1 below.

Extensive interviewing was conducted both at corporate level and at the unit of analysis with senior decision makers, first line managers/team leaders and front-line employees (such as financial consultants and sales associates). These latter interviews were structured using an administered questionnaire (with control questions from the Workplace Employee Relations Survey 1998) and sought to explore how people management practices impact on employee attitudes and behaviour. They were repeated after 12 months to allow us to track changes that were taking place both at an organisational level and in the unit of analysis.

We believe that one of the strengths of this research are these individual face-to-face interviews with employees (in other words, those at whom the practices are aimed), which allowed us to provide a fairly accurate assessment of the impact of the HR practices that exist in the unit. The multiple-respondents design enabled us to uncover differences between stated policies and the implementation of those policies. The interview data was examined alongside performance data (financial, operational and HR measures) and information on the HR policies for the unit of analysis.

Further details on the research design are provided in Appendix 1, and a brief summary of the case studies is at Annexe A to Appendix 1.

The structure of the report

Chapter 2 introduces one of the key concepts by focusing on values and wider organisation issues – what we call the Big Idea – and the way these inform choices in HR management. We provide some data and give illustrations for some of our organisations which clearly had strong cultures and where the Big Idea spread through the organisation. This allows us to explore some of the case organisations in some depth and use the questionnaire results to show what works, and why.

Increasingly, as we did the research, we came to realise that a crucial variable is how policies, practices and values are brought to life, or stifled.

Table 1 | Case-study organisations

Organisation	Unit of analysis	Number of employees in survey	
		Year 1	Year 2
AIT	Whole organisation, project teams	36	33
Contact 24	Four customer service teams	33	40
Clerical Medical	Clerical/admin staff in customer services	29	34
Jaguar	Manual workers in Trim and Assembly	41	37
Nationwide Building Society	Sales force, southern region	44	49
Oxford Magnetic Technology (OMT)	Magnetic design engineers and assembly workers	40	40
PriceWaterhouseCoopers	Accountants, ABAS south	43	27
Royal Mint	Manual workers in MRB department	42	33
Royal United Hospital, Bath	Clinical department (nurses, technicians, porters)	40	39
Selfridges	Sales associates, Trafford centre store, Manchester	40	41
Siemens Medical	Field service engineers/ national technical support engineers and call centre staff	27	–
Tesco	Section managers in four stores	43	40

Understanding the People and Performance Link: Unlocking the black box | **11**

How can we explain the connection between people management and performance?

This is where the role of line managers, especially the immediate team leader with direct, daily responsibility for employees is so important. This is the topic of Chapter 3.

Chapter 4 looks at performance – what measures are important, how these are collected and interpreted – and assesses, as far as the analysis is able to at this stage, the link between people management and performance. What is interesting here is how few organisations, even the sophisticated ones, really bother to prove the connection on a regular basis. The chapter goes on to look at the issue of sustaining performance.

Chapter 5 begins to bring everything together. It does so by using the questionnaire data in the two projects collected by interviewing 1,000+ people to find the drivers of organisation commitment, motivation and job satisfaction. We look at three occupational groups: team leaders/front line managers, professionals and workers.

Finally, in Chapter 6 we draw together all of our findings and ask what are the implications for HR professionals.

2 | The Big Idea: integrating HR strategy and practice with the business

The Big Idea: overview

One of the most notable features of some of our research organisations was the existence of what we came to call the Big Idea. The Big Idea is a clear sense of mission underpinned by values and a culture expressing what the firm is and its relationship with its customers and employees.

There are five key attributes to the Big Idea as revealed in the research.

Embedded

First, the Big Idea is not necessarily captured in a formal mission statement agreed at the board level but exists rather as values that are spread throughout the organisation. In our interviews at all levels we kept hearing references to these values and to the underlying organisation culture, not always expressed in the same terms, but clearly deriving from a common root. That is, they were embedded into organisational practice. These values and the way they are expressed by different people in different ways in the same firm are a long way beyond trite statements like 'Our employees are our most important resources.'

Connected

Second, these values which indicated what sort of organisation the firm sought to be interconnected the relationships with customers and the organisational culture and behaviour, and thus set the fundamentals on how employees should be managed, and their responsibilities to each other, and to customers. This link between HR and customers – the internal and the external – meant that values were consistent and mutually reinforcing between, for example, HR and marketing. This was particularly evident in customer-facing organisations like Selfridges, Tesco

and Nationwide, where the logic of the employee-customer-profit chain applied.

The most famous example of this is the US chain store Sears, where strong evidence exists that the organisation became 'a compelling place to invest' when it was seen as a 'compelling place to shop' and was recognised as 'a compelling place to work' (Rucci, Kirn and Quinn, 1998).

Enduring

Third, these values, at their best, were enduring and provided a stable base on which different initiatives and policies could be built and changed as circumstances altered. Strong enduring values, historically derived (sometimes known as 'path dependency'), provided the basis both for the management of performance and the achievement of change. It is a form of historical learning at the organisational level.

This was particularly important in sustaining performance and flexibility, but was sometimes hard to achieve. In one of our organisations, growing pressure for cost containment was perceived by employees to weaken commitment to core values about people. In other cases values remained clear and strong, and this was reflected in enduring commitment by employees to their organisation even when difficult decisions had to be made.

Collective

Fourth, the Big Idea has the attributes of strong cultures where the organisational culture is a sort of glue binding people and processes together. It is thus a collective endeavour and differs from HR policies in its effect in linking people management to performance.

> ' Values ... provide the extra ingredients that can mark
> out superior sustained performance: what is referred
> to as "organisational process advantage".'

Most HR policies are, of necessity, focused on the individual employee – selection, appraisal, pay, training and development, communication, work–life balance, etc – and the individualisation of the employment contract has encouraged this. The outcome of these HR policies, if properly designed and applied, will increase the human capital pool and provide continuous replacement. This provides the human resource advantage. Values, and in a different sense organisational routines – how work is done – provide the extra ingredients that can mark out superior sustained performance: what is referred to as 'organisational process advantage'.

Some organisations develop high levels of efficiencies through the creation and continuous refinement of excellent routines so that everyone knows what to do and how to do it, time and again. Good examples in our organisations were Jaguar, Tesco, and Nationwide. In Nationwide's case, part of the need for routines was the need to satisfy the regulatory requirements in the financial services industry. This collective endeavour, the ability to join people together in one common goal, is reinforced by underlying values about the dominant purpose of the organisation, the way it treats customers and employees.

Successful organisations thus combine, in unique ways, values, routines and policy-practice which affect both individuals and the collective endeavour. It is this 'social complexity' which is so hard to copy. Individual HR policies can easily be replicated but it is the mix of these policies with well developed routines underpinned by values collectively applied and embedded that is so hard to imitate.

Measured and managed

In a number of cases a balanced scorecard (Kaplan and Norton, 1996) or the 'tomorrow's company'

approach (Goyder, 1998) was used not just as a means of measuring performance in four or five attributes of the business (typically shareholders, customers, employees, operational excellence, and in some the community) but as a means of integrating different functional areas and decisions into linked processes. This integration was both vertical – linking the top with the bottom – and horizontal – interconnecting HR with marketing, for example, and with operations across the functional areas.

In one case when the balanced scorecard just generated performance numbers discussed at a monthly management board meeting, it was much less effective than in those cases where processes were integrated, informing and influencing decision-making, and where these decisions were themselves deeply influenced by values associated with the Big Idea.

The Big Idea and its link with employee commitment to the organisation

The existence of the Big Idea in some of our research organisations is, of necessity, something that the researchers had to measure subjectively in trying to isolate those organisations that had distinct elements that met the criteria of 'embedded', 'connected', 'enduring', 'collective' and 'measured and managed'. The five organisations shown in Figure 2 all had clearly articulated a Big Idea that had been in existence for some time, and four of the five had a balanced scorecard or had adopted the methodology of the 'tomorrow's organisation' approach.

The exception was Jaguar, but it had – through the Ford Production System (FPS) and the use of advanced quality management called 6-Sigma – extensive measures that were interrelated one with the other.

Figure 2 shows the mean scores (based on a five-point scale in which 5 is strongly agree, 1 is strongly disagree) for two of the questions testing organisational commitment from Year 1 of our survey. These questions were derived from WERS 1998.[1] The data allows us to compare our organisations with the national average. All six of the organisations in Figure 2 exceeded this. The average for all employees in the remaining six case-study organisations is shown in the bottom two bars. All six organisations with a clearly articulated Big Idea and with the use of some form of balanced scorecard were above average in most or all of the questions.

To get a more accurate comparison, we found, in the WERS data bank, the nearest equivalent occupational group in the appropriate sector. For example, we compared the Selfridges sales associates with retail trade sales staff, and Nationwide financial sales consultants with sales employees in the financial intermediaries sector. Again all outperformed their comparators. However, this was not true amongst the remaining six organisations, two of which were below the national average for their comparator.

Figure 2 | Measures of organisational commitment – first-year interviews, mean scores
5-point scale on which 5 is 'strongly agree', 1 is 'strongly disagree'

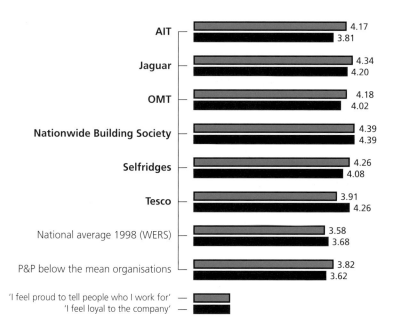

AIT	4.17	3.81
Jaguar	4.34	4.20
OMT	4.18	4.02
Nationwide Building Society	4.39	4.39
Selfridges	4.26	4.08
Tesco	3.91	4.26
National average 1998 (WERS)	3.58	3.68
P&P below the mean organisations	3.82	3.62

'I feel proud to tell people who I work for'
'I feel loyal to the company'

1 The Workplace Employee Relations Survey (WERS) 1998 is based on large samples which are representative of the great majority of workplaces in Great Britain, and involves interviews with managers, employee representatives and employees. The data used here is based on employee responses.

> **'... there is strong evidence in these six organisations that the existence of a Big Idea ... was reflected in the commitment employees showed to their organisations.'**

In other words there is strong evidence in these six organisations that the existence of a Big Idea or mission/culture/values articulation which is embedded and interconnected, and which is linked with a means to measure and integrate, was reflected in the commitment employees showed to their organisations. Organisational commitment was high in each of these organisations.

What did the Big Idea mean in practice? Here we give a short sketch of five organisations and use the attitude survey to provide more evidence.

Nationwide Building Society

Nationwide puts members first, by providing a range of top-value quality financial services that are widely available and delivered with speed, courtesy and reliability – backed by policies of fairness, honesty, staff importance and corporate responsibility. After a detailed strategic review, the Society has decided that the best commercial route to deliver this proposition is to remain a building society.
– Nationwide member proposition, 2001

The above proposition, based around principles of fairness and putting the customer first, and a commitment to staying mutual, clearly sets out the Nationwide approach to business which it has sought to pursue in a high-profile campaign in recent years. The idea of 'mutuality' as a key value deeply influences the way the Society manages relationships with its customers and its employers.

Nationwide's commitment to mutuality back in 1995 resulted in the development of a new business strategy to improve customer services and streamline operations, and has enabled the Society to develop a unique position in the financial services market place. The Society has increasingly promoted itself as champion of the consumer in the personal financial market (a recent example being the campaign to abolish cash machine charges), delivering member value through its mutual strategy and providing a real alternative to the banks. By putting the customer first, rather than the shareholder, the Society is able to operate on narrower margins (compared to the converted building societies) and reduced planned profit so that customers receive long-term benefits by way of improved rates and better services.

Part of the new business strategy in 1995 included the establishment of new performance measures around three key criteria:

- ◘ the customer

- ◘ the business

- ◘ the employees,

thus:

- ◘ 'Nationwide is my first choice.'

- ◘ 'Nationwide has the best ratings.'

- ◘ 'Nationwide is where I want to work.'

Key performance indicators – or KPIs – which are set annually, initially at corporate level (based on the three-year plan), are used to measure performance against these criteria. So, for example, employee satisfaction (based on the employee attitude survey) and competence are used as indicators of 'Nationwide is where I want to work'; mortgage share and complaints are included in measures of 'Nationwide is my first choice'; capital ratios, costs and controls reflect the statement 'Nationwide has the best ratings'. These measures are not weighted and all have equal value.

KPIs are also an effective communication process – as the planning manager observed:

One of the advantages of these performance measures is that they have engaged people lower down the organisation with the corporate objectives.

The whole planning process is managed by the Group planning department, which develops the corporate plan (which runs from April to March) after consultation with all divisional directors and the board. Each division then develops its own plan with a steer from the planning department. Each plan is documented and progress-assessed using a traffic lights system of red, amber and green balls, and progress can be monitored via the intranet site.

In the branches, targets are set by the divisional director of the branch network based around a complex financial planning model produced at head office. Ultimately these measures are based on targets in the corporate plan.

Branch and area team performance is measured against seven core targets, each of which has been allocated different weighting according to its importance. Various team-based reward systems are linked to these targets, paid in various ways like reward vouchers and team events. One ex-branch manager explained:

It's all about recognition rather than reward.

Recent internal research by Nationwide has confirmed the interconnection between levels of positive staff attitudes and measures of customer satisfaction at the branch level – ie at the point of delivery. This focus on customer-based performance driven through people, products and

processes led to a Group-wide campaign launched in 2002 called PRIDE (standing for Putting the people first, Rising to the challenge, Inspiring confidence, Delivering better value, Exceeding expectations).

Our unit of analysis, suggested by the organisation, was the sales force in the Southern region. The sales force, established in the early 1990s, has grown from 250 to around 350 financial consultants (plus 65 supervisory staff) over the past five years as the product range has increased.

The majority who work in retail sales are financial consultants (FCs) who work as part of a branch team but are linked in FC teams organised on a geographical basis. The FCs are based in branch offices where most sales leads originate.

The Society has used a wide variety of HR policies to support the long-term strategy of mutuality and to develop an integrated loyal sales force. For example, in terms of recruitment and selection, internal applicants are preferred for cultural reasons (currently 90 per cent of applicants to the sales force are internal). As one senior manager explained:

Culture is very important … we want people to behave in the right way. There tends to be a higher turnover in externally recruited staff partly because their ethics don't fit or they are not good at relationship-building and not part of the Nationwide culture.

When recruiting externally, Nationwide favours inexperienced people rather than experienced financial consultants, who are normally motivated largely by money rather than the customer. As another manager explained:

> ' **Nationwide ... has been able to generate high levels of commitment, motivation and job satisfaction.'**

We want to attract those whose main interest is in putting the customer first, then Nationwide, and then reward, and our adverts reflect this. But if you look at competitors' adverts, earnings always come first.

Reward is based on collective as well as individual performance. Many other financial institutions selling similar products have emphasised individual performance, sometimes by using self-employed consultants/advisers. In more recent years a good number of organisations have withdrawn from such direct sales activities due to increased regulation from the FSA and falling revenue.

The different approach of Nationwide, albeit facing difficulties caused by a change in its discount mortgage policy, would appear to be reflected in the attitudes of its sales force. It has been able to generate high levels of commitment,

motivation and job satisfaction. One financial consultant we interviewed put it this way:

I believe in mutuality and putting the customer before profits. They pay us well to avoid unethical selling. I'm here for life!'

This attitude is illustrated in Table 2, which correlates staff evaluations of certain HR practices with these attitudinal outcomes. We show here the results from the first-year interviews and return to the second year later when we address the sustainability in the discussion on performance.

It is not surprising in a sales force to find that pay satisfaction linked to job satisfaction, motivation and commitment, and, for professionals like these, satisfaction with career opportunities and appraisal (knowing how well you are doing and getting advice on how to improve) are also important. The

Table 2 | The relationship between employee evaluations of HR practices and attitudinal outcomes: Nationwide first-year correlations (n = 43)

	Job satisfaction	Motivation	Commitment
Job security	*	*	*
Training			*
Career opportunity	*		**
Appraisal	*		**
Pay satisfaction	**	**	*
Job challenge			
Teamworking			
Involvement	*	*	*
Communication	**	*	**
Openness (ability to raise concerns)	*		*
Work–life balance	*		**
Management behaviour	**	*	

** significant at .01 level (2-tailed)[2]
 * significant at .05 level (2-tailed)

[2] .01 level of significance equates to 99 per cent confidence that this relationship does not occur by chance.

fact that Nationwide is prepared to invest in training and development is reflected in the link with organisational commitment.

What is particularly interesting in this case are the additional drivers of attitudinal outcomes, especially people's sense of having opportunities to be involved, to know about plans and prospects (communication), the perceived openness of the Society in allowing concerns to be raised and generally in the behaviour of front-line managers. As we note in the next chapter, this throws particular light on the role of front-line leadership. These latter 'HR practices' are not concrete policies enshrined and defined in a manual. They are management behaviours and are a clear indication of the values of 'mutuality' in action.

Selfridges plc

Since the mid-1990s Selfridges has embarked on an ambitious renewal and growth programme. During this time the critical strategic choice has been about what sort of retailer Selfridges should be and how internal staff management would be linked into this. The need was to recruit and develop staff who had deep product knowledge and were able to create relationships with customers. The widespread view was that customers were becoming much more discerning than they had been, and increasingly wanted an enjoyable experience beyond the simple transaction of buying. Staff, especially staff associates who serve customers, were seen to be central to creating and achieving this ambience and experience. The creation of a 'store for the next century' – as Vittorio Radice, the chief executive, demanded – required a major change in almost every aspect of the business, including:

◘ integrated IT systems linking suppliers to Selfridges, and improved communication within the organisation

◘ a new team of retail operations managers meeting weekly

◘ a new approach to buying such that buyers have been taken off the department floor and no longer report to a senior manager in the department

◘ a change to seven-days-a-week trading, with longer opening hours (till 9 pm in Trafford Park, but for four months around the turn of the year, till 10 pm)

◘ a new approach to leadership and management style, now required to be 'aspirational, friendly and accessible' – although many thought it had really become rather 'aggressive' in practice

◘ the assumption by managers of responsibility for people management (previously even first-level disciplinary matters had been referred to the personnel department)

◘ new and more accurate performance measures, especially in relation to profit per square foot, and data on 'foot-fall' and KPIs – this financial information and data was to be made available down to the lowest level so that 'economic literacy' would improve

◘ a different, more partnership-based relationship with concessionaires and their staff.

' ... every member of staff is reviewed according to a development plan with the aim of trying to maximise people's talents and fitting their careers around these strengths.'

Most of all, Selfridges had to move from the simple provision of customer service to being customer-friendly, and beyond that to becoming customer-driven. The commercial controller stated the case succinctly:

Selfridges see themselves at the upper end of the price market, with customers prepared to pay a little bit more – so the service must be good. People will be critical to that.

Selfridges trades as the 'House of brands', with a strong brand image of its own based around that general concept. Early in the transformation, the HR director told us, they consciously set out to change the internal brand image of Selfridges amongst the staff, making it identical to the revitalised external brand image.

Culture surveys were undertaken, focus groups were organised amongst staff, a new 360-degree or 180-degree appraisal system was introduced. The old Hay job evaluation system was thrown out in favour of a broadbanded pay arrangement that replaced age or length of service with performance-based progression. A new staff council was created that included union representatives from USDAW. Staff representatives were encouraged to head up project teams on such topics as clothing allowances, facilities and the staff restaurant. NVQs for sales associates were introduced, also involving financial rewards for advancement. More care was taken with selection and promotion.

Within the Trafford Park store, where we did our fieldwork, they introduced six-monthly assessment performance reviews (APRs). In the period September to October every member of staff is reviewed according to a development plan with the aim of trying to maximise people's talents and fitting their careers around these strengths. In

February a second review takes place which is more closely linked to pay and performance bonuses.

There is a widespread use of the 'mystery shopper', who reports on the staff's customer-centred skills. The company acronym for such presentation skills is SHINE (standing for Smile, Help, Inform, New product push, End the sale). Many of the staff associates we interviewed had been 'mystery shopped', and there was a general acceptance that this was the way in which Selfridges encourages performance.

Every day, and at the beginning of the late shift, there is a 10-minute briefing break. Each month there is a more formal communication event called Team Talk Time. This might, for example, be about the Save-As-You-Earn scheme that is linked to share purchase, as it was on the one day we were doing the research. Training is provided at the end of the week in the morning, and also at the weekend.

Behind all these innovations in HR and in its link with other aspects of the business – a very good example of best fit and best process – there was an explicit effort to feature the underlying stakeholder values required in their dealings with customers, employees, the community, suppliers and stakeholders. The values as expressed are shown in Figure 3. The goal is 'to turn values into value' by acting out those values.

The values are expressed in a more articulated form under three goals:

Selfridges should be
**aspirational,
friendly, and
bold.**

Under each of the stakeholder value headings a question is raised about the values required.

◧ Employee values: *How does this make me want to work here?*

◧ Customer values: *How am I encouraged to shop?*

◧ Community values: *How does Selfridges reflect the spirit of the city?*

◧ Shareholder values: *Why should we invest in the store?*

◧ Supplier values: *What makes Selfridges an interesting proposition?*

Figure 3 | The Selfridge stakeholder value model

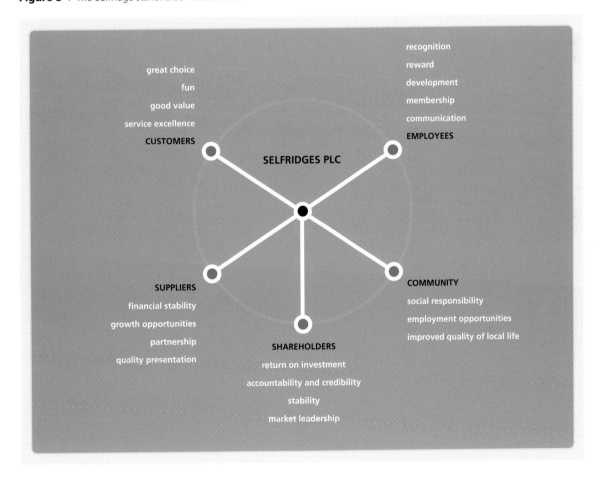

Table 3 gives an example of how these questions are to be answered in terms of aspirations under the general banner of 'Friendly: everyone is welcome'.

These are bold value statements, and the development of HR architecture was innovative in trying to turn them into reality. There were, and are, real challenges in making this work.

The long opening hours meant that staff had to be found for weekends and evenings, and that key staff had to work on a rota basis. Such scheduling broke with the traditional working patterns in Manchester at the time. It was not helped by the fact that the public transport system was poor, especially at the end of the evening shift, so that travel to and from work caused problems. This made it hard to find and to keep staff. Staff

Table 3 | Selfridges: an example of the values matrix – 'Friendly: everyone is welcome'

Employee values: – how does this make me want to work here?	Selfridges is a very friendly place to work. I like my boss and my team.	I know my opinion and contribution is welcomed.	I feel welcomed and this makes me welcome others.
Customer values: – how am I encouraged to shop?	People at Selfridges are always smiling and helpful – they seem to enjoy working there.	I like to buy and browse in Selfridges – I never feel under pressure, but rarely come home empty-handed.	Selfridges represents the good things about city living.
Community values: – how does Selfridges reflect the spirit of the city?	Selfridges promotes an inclusive spirit.	It is a microcosm of all the different cultures and communities that make up the city.	Through its managers and staff Selfridges gets involved in community projects.
Shareholder values: – why should we invest in the store?	Selfridges' annual reports are inviting and easy to read.	Selfridges' financial information is transparent, and the directors are open to any questions.	I feel welcome when I attend shareholders' meetings.
Supplier values: – what makes Selfridges an interesting proposition?	We help each other in the continuous improvement of our relationship.	Selfridges' wide and diverse range of quality products adds value to my product.	My concession staff are treated well and made to feel welcome.

' **Selfridges staff ... had one of the highest levels of organisational commitment of any of our 12 organisations.'**

turnover was high, particularly in the first few years after opening the Manchester store, although less than the normal for the retail trade. (The organisation subsequently successfully reduced turnover from 78 per cent in 2000 to 40 per cent in 2001.)

There remains a heavy reliance on part-time staff. In these circumstances it is more expensive to develop a sophisticated HR system.

An added complication is that as the 'House of brands' a large proportion of the sales associates are concessionary staff. As shown in Table 3, the suppliers' values statement claims that 'My concession staff are treated well and made to feel welcome.' In practice this means that concession staff join sales teams and take part in communication activities. There were no major differences between the views of concessionary staff and those of Selfridges employees in our survey, and 92 per cent of our respondents felt that the relationship between Selfridges staff and concessionary staff was good.

Selfridges staff (including the concessionary staff) had one of the highest levels of organisational commitment of any of our 12 organisations. Indeed, in terms of a comparison with the attitudes of retail trade staff nationally, taken from the WERS 98 survey, the level was markedly better.

For example, figures from our first-year survey show:

- 97 per cent are proud to tell people who they work for (WERS 98: 56 per cent)

- 93 per cent are loyal to Selfridges (WERS 98: 70 per cent)

- 83 per cent would recommend a friend or relative to work in Selfridges

- 72 per cent say they share the values of the organisation (WERS 98: 50 per cent).

Looking at the correlations (Table 4), it is clear that what was really important in Year 1 in linking into commitment, motivation and job satisfaction were aspects of the job. Vital in this respect were job challenge and teamworking, the feeling that the job was secure and that there were career opportunities linked with appraisal, and most of all, satisfaction with the degree and style of communication, levels of involvement and the way managers managed. The key design features of the HR system are clearly reflected in this bundle of people management practices.

One of the written values is 'Selfridges is a store where there are many career opportunities'. Satisfaction with these opportunities for those who wanted them was clear in the survey, and this fed through into motivation and commitment.

Another written aspiration in the value statement is 'I like my boss and my team, and I know my opinion and contribution is welcomed'. These sentiments too are reflected in our survey under teamworking, involvement and management behaviour, and in the opportunity to raise a concern, which is a test of openness.

Table 4 | The relationship between HR practices and employee attitudes in Selfridges – first-year correlation results (n = 40)

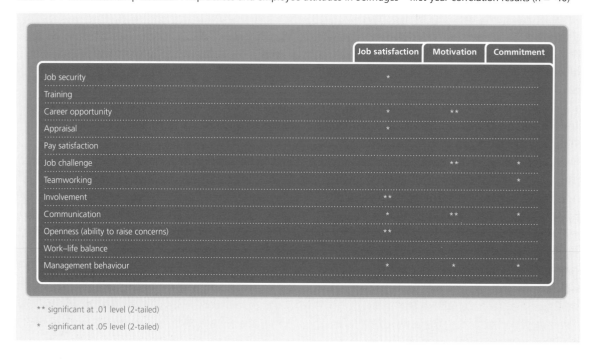

	Job satisfaction	Motivation	Commitment
Job security	*		
Training			
Career opportunity	*	**	
Appraisal	*		
Pay satisfaction			
Job challenge		**	*
Teamworking			*
Involvement	**		
Communication	*	**	*
Openness (ability to raise concerns)	**		
Work–life balance			
Management behaviour	*	*	*

** significant at .01 level (2-tailed)

* significant at .05 level (2-tailed)

Of course, nothing is perfect. One of the problems with value statements, if they are to mean anything, is that they raise expectations. In the first-year survey, 46 per cent of those interviewed said they wanted more recognition and appreciation shown by management, and two-thirds said they were hardly ever asked by managers for their views.

As one respondent put it:

Management should have a more relaxed, approachable attitude … do more floor-work, and ask staff what problems they have. They should be more involved on the shop floor.

What the correlations show is that those staff who were satisfied with their manager and the way they were managed had high levels of commitment, motivation and job satisfaction.

Since it was the managers who undertook the daily and monthly communication sessions, and it was these managers who did the appraisals, the strong correlations here in these segments also reflect management style and management behaviour. The problem was, according to our respondents, that there were just not enough managers undertaking this type of people management to the level expected by the staff. As we note in Chapter 3, this is an important part of people management – and Selfridges took this on board as a result of our first-year feedback.

The importance of the line manager in delivering people management comes out even more clearly when we look more closely at the drivers of commitment, motivation and job satisfaction. For example, those who felt they received a lot of coaching and guidance from their line manager were much more likely to show commitment to

> ' **Quality is not just an outcome seen in product reliability, design and build, it is also about processes and routines.** '

Selfridges, and this was true too if they thought management was good at dealing with absenteeism and lateness. The managers' active role was also linked to people's sense of having a career opportunity and their satisfaction with the appraisal system.

In that the managers we are referring to were mainly team leaders (the immediate line manager), there was not surprisingly also a link with the staff's satisfaction with teamworking.

Jaguar Cars

The Big Idea in Jaguar is quality. The organisation's position in the JD Power league table and other consumer tests is just one part of it, albeit it crucial for performance in the market place.

Quality is not just an outcome seen in product reliability, design and build, it is also about processes and routines. It drives down costs by reducing reworking, eliminating the need for an army of quality inspectors, and minimising accidents and injuries.

This latter issue is a major focus at the Browns Lane plant in Coventry, where we did our research, because the workforce is long established (a third of those we interviewed were aged over 50) and with outsourcing of some areas it was harder to move people off the track to different, slower jobs.

Thus the pursuit of quality has many meanings and many outcomes. Everyone in the plant we talked to recognised the need for quality. The unions raise quality issues with senior management in their regular meetings, and workers had pride in the product. Said one operative:

'I did that one' is a good feeling as a Jaguar goes by on the road.

Ford took over Jaguar in 1989. The recession of the early 1990s led to major difficulties involving large-scale redundancies, many of which were compulsory. The union officers still remember that time with horror.

Sitting down with senior managers to decide who was going to be made compulsorily redundant was very painful. We decided we did not want it to happen again.

A flexibility deal was agreed then with the unions, and they have subsequently worked in partnership with the organisation helping to bring in quality measures while still keeping their distance and independence when they feel it necessary.

One aspect of quality has been the use of metrics to measure everything and to identify appropriate actions. ('We have figures like dogs have fleas,' said one senior manager.) Such efforts have usually been presented as 'eleven steps' or 'eight goals' or 'seven plus one wastes'. (Interestingly, the eighth waste is 'under-utilisation of our people, their skills and knowledge'.)

These metrics are linked with the typical hardware of lean production systems, as described in an earlier CIPD report (Hutchinson et al, 1998): statistical process control (SPC), value-stream analysis (VSA) with value-stream mapping (VSM), Ford Total Preventive Maintenance (FTPM), and so on. Most of these measures are Ford-driven and provide benchmark standards across the Group but especially within Ford Europe and the Premier Automotive Group which now includes Volvo and Landrover.

The success of these quality initiatives and the launch of new models have led to a substantial expansion in the Jaguar manufacturing capacity involving the opening of the new, revitalised old

Ford Halewood plant on Merseyside, and with further capacity at Castle Bromwich.

As Jaguar recovered and retooled in the 1990s with the help of Ford investment and Ford management expertise, the most important of these quality measures was Q1, the Ford Quality Standard. This standard was mandatory. At first Jaguar was bottom of the league. But by the time we did our interviews in 2000 they were top – even getting accusations from other Ford plants that they must be fiddling the data because no plant could be that good.

That year Jaguar also won the JD Power Gold Award for the best-quality plant in Europe (shared with Porsche). Since then there has been the progressive adoption of the Ford Production System (FPS) covering all aspects of work in great detail, and the introduction of 6-Sigma, a quality management tool involving project focus and analysis, using trained employees full time on this work for two years (the black belts) and part-time team members (brown belts). Quite a number of brown belts are manual workers, and it is not unusual for manual workers to meet suppliers as part of problem-solving.

The people management dimensions of the pursuit of quality are not to be found in a battery of new HR policies. In some ways there is a continuity in the basics of HR. People queue up for jobs in Jaguar, although it was only until very recently with the new model launch that there was any need to recruit. Training in quality standards is necessary, but there is no appraisal system, no performance pay and no attitude surveys or suchlike for manual workers on the line.

Communication is important about quality problems and the meeting of targets, but beyond

that it has proved difficult to get it right in terms of wider plant issues. Quite a few of the people we talked to had no memory of the annual talk given by the managing director each year!

What is important, however, is the reorganisation of employees on the track and in the trim shop into teams. One of their number is chosen by management as team leader, known as a group leader, and paid a supplement. There remains some resistance to this – some of the older employees thinking of group leaders as 'gaffers' narks' – but the team leaders themselves whom we interviewed were positive and enthusiastic. Eventually there will be a ratio of one group leader to eight employees and groups will become more self-managing – for example, doing their own job timing and work study. This is a form of empowerment to some, but is not particularly welcomed by others.

Already teams do their own quality measures, enter data on to charts in the team area, spot variances, undertake statistical analysis and take corrective action, all as part of SPC. Group leaders enter issues on the Counter-Measure Boards on behalf of the team. There are set time limits for a management response.

Some middle managers find it hard to deal with this sort of employee involvement. As the production manager puts it:

The real skill is learning how to say no and explaining it, if no is the correct answer.

Initially, when group leaders were introduced, the track stopped at 11 am each Friday for 15 minutes to discuss issues on quality, cost, health and safety and employment matters, and so on. Now the track stops once a day for five minutes, with a set

' **"Measurement" and "ownership" come through frequently in our interview notes with senior managers and with group leaders as the key processes in achieving quality.**'

topic for each day. Teams also now do routine maintenance as part of FTPM. Some see this as work intensification, others as empowerment by which group leaders have a key role in work allocations dealing with quality and communication and 'owning' the work processes.

Such a focus on 'ownership' has influenced how new production lines and new models are introduced. In the mid-1990s an innovative line was installed by a specialist design team, but it turned out to be defective. The people who were to work on that line were not consulted. This was, according to the production director, 'a really hard lesson', and led to the idea that people had to be involved in both big things and little things in order to achieve the level of quality which Jaguar had to reach.

'Measurement' and 'ownership' come through frequently in our interview notes with senior managers and with group leaders as the key processes in achieving quality.

We interviewed 41 manual workers in the first year, mainly from track and assembly but some from the trim shop; 37 were interviewed in the second year. Compared with the national data for manufacturing operatives taken from WERS 98,

◘ there was a higher level of job satisfaction – 64 per cent compared with 52 per cent

◘ and very high levels of commitment – 95 per cent being proud to tell people who they worked for, compared with 47 per cent nationally

◘ 85 per cent felt loyal to the organisation (WERS 98: 55 per cent).

The underlying historically derived commitment to Jaguar and its distinctive green logo, as opposed to the blue oval of Ford, as a representation of value, provided a strong base for people management. That was the case even when a large number of respondents felt they had to work very hard, and when double the number in the WERS survey worried about their job outside work. Three-quarters of our respondents said that their sense of teamworking was very or fairly strong, and an equal number felt that membership of teams helped them improve their performance. It is important to recall that teams were introduced only relatively recently.

When we asked about employees' attitudes to their managers, respondents felt it was important to differentiate between the levels of management. The key management level was the immediate manager, and many people included the group leader as one of these people even though group leaders are manual workers and have no formal management responsibility for such things as discipline. Higher-level management began at the level of the superintendent.

In respect of their immediate manager:

◘ 61 per cent felt managers were good at dealing with problems (WERS 98: 33 per cent)

◘ 68 per cent felt managers were good at treating employees fairly (WERS 98: 35 per cent).

Commitment was particularly (and significantly) associated with people's good experience of teamworking, involvement and communication. The other main links, also seen in the way they helped trigger job satisfaction and motivation, were people's satisfaction with their training and

> ' **The introduction of this approach brought about a ...
> change in culture which is seen as a major catalyst for
> Tesco's recent success.'**

development, the career opportunities they had, and their job challenge. This was especially true for group leaders themselves, who were much more positive than other manual workers belonging to their team. However, where workers felt their immediate managers actively provided help and guidance in their jobs, they were more likely to show high levels of commitment to Jaguar and to find their jobs satisfying.

The new organisational form of teams and group leaders was affirmed in our results. Although work intensification had occurred, it was interestingly those who found their jobs challenging who were more likely to express strong commitment to the firm and to have higher levels of job satisfaction. In this case the values associated with working for a high-quality leading car manufacturer were translated into commitment and job satisfaction, especially when the relationship with immediate line management was good, and where people felt they had a challenging job, beyond the monotony of the line, and had training and development to help them with their job and career aspirations.

To them, working for Jaguar was more than just doing a job each and every day. All this was especially true for group leaders, manual workers on the first rung of management

Tesco

Tesco, the UK's largest food retailer, in order to improve its competitive position, underwent considerable change in the mid-1990s by placing much greater emphasis on a customer-facing culture. As one senior head office manager remarked:

1995 saw the evolution of a customer-focused business ... With quality and price being very

much the same across the sector, people and our service were seen as the differentiator.

Together with Gemini consultants, Tesco developed its own version of the balanced scorecard (Kaplan and Norton, 1996) to help define their business more strongly and bring about this culture change. The scorecard was translated into a 'steering wheel' with four quadrants – people, finance, customers and operations – and each store's performance is measured against specific targets in each area.

In the people quadrant, for example, targets include recruitment, development, retention, absence and staff morale (taken from their staff attitude survey).

Although the four quadrants are not weighted, one retail director we interviewed considered the people quadrant to be the most important. He explained:

If we can recruit, maintain and deliver fantastic people, then operationally we can deliver.

The measures are updated each quarter and link to the corporate measures which underpin the organisation's strategic objectives. In each store there is a large 'steering wheel' on display, which is highly visible to staff who can monitor their own store's performance using a traffic-lights system (red, green and amber to show if performance is below, above, or on target).

The introduction of this approach brought about a much greater focus on people and customer issues in the stores, which historically had been driven by financial and operational results, and a consequent change in culture which is seen as a major catalyst for Tesco's recent success.

De-layering took place as part of the restructuring exercise. Within the stores there are currently four levels: store manager, senior managers, section managers and general assistants. Each store is run by a store manager whose job it is to provide coaching, guidance and support, and to deliver the Tesco 'standard'.

As one store manager explained:

My role is to mobilise the team with a goal, to be energetic, and to be able to motivate people.

There is a senior management team in each store made up of operational managers responsible for departments and, in an average-sized store (employing around 400 staff) this would comprise five or six managers who might typically include the store manager, the personnel manager, the customer services manager, the fresh foods/ambient manager and an out-of-hours manager. Each member of this team, including the personnel manager, takes a turn in managing the store for around 20 per cent of his or her working time so as to gain an understanding of the business issues.

The personnel function within the stores (over two-thirds of stores have their own personnel manager) has undergone considerable change over the past five or six years, moving from a predominantly administrative and welfare role to a store-level senior management position. The role of the personnel manager includes responsibility for the payroll and controllable expenses, and for ensuring that the store maintains productivity levels. This means focusing on the people measures within the 'steering wheel' – such as absence management, employee appraisal and development, resourcing and succession planning. One of the benefits of the steering wheel has therefore been to make the role of the personnel manager much clearer within the stores, and to

enable the function to measure itself against specific goals.

A more recent change within Tesco has been the drive for consistency across stores. All policies, procedures and processes are centrally determined and their implementation closely monitored. Every store is governed by the organisation's routines handbook, which provides detailed information on how every task is to be performed – down to the minutest detail, even on office layout, such as where pictures should go on the wall, and where the waste-paper bin should go!

On the HR side, all policies and procedures are highly centralised and controlled. The wages budget, for example, is fixed for each store and there is very little local flexibility on pay – something which was obviously a cause of great frustration in some of the stores we visited, where recruitment, retention and staff quality were on-going major problems.

Although the stores cannot function without these routines, it is the way the rules and routines are implemented that is considered a key ingredient to success. One store manager explained:

It is management – in particular, the general manager – who are responsible for how the policies and processes are implemented, and their behaviour is therefore critical to a store's performance.

This is borne out by the preliminary results from Year 1 of our research, and explained more fully in Chapter 3.

Our research focused on the section manager population, which is a first-line manager position within the store. Spans of control are normally 12

> ' **Tesco section managers scored highest of all our case-study organisations in terms of working hard...'**

general assistants to each section manager, and in an average-sized store there may be about 20 section managers covering such different areas as produce, bakery, non- food, and checkout. In addition to being responsible for the day-to-day running of their areas, section managers take responsibility for a range of people management tasks such as recruitment, training, performance appraisal, disciplinary and grievance issues, and pay enquiries. The nature of the job is therefore fairly demanding – particularly on the people management side – and this may partly explain why many stores face recruitment and retention difficulties with this position.

Interestingly, like staff in the other retail organisation in our study (Selfridges), Tesco section managers displayed one of the highest levels of organisational commitment of any of our case-study organisations, and were highest in terms of sharing the values of the organisation. Comparisons with the WERS 98 survey data for retail trade staff also show that Tesco's staff had significantly higher levels of commitment.

- 74 per cent felt proud to tell people who they worked for (WERS 98: 56 per cent)

- 88 per cent felt loyal to Tesco (WERS 98: 70 per cent)

- 86 per cent would recommend a friend or relative to work in Tesco

- 88 per cent say they share the values of Tesco (WERS 98: 50 per cent).

This is particularly interesting, given that Tesco section managers scored highest of all our case-study organisations in terms of working hard (91 per cent felt they worked very hard), and were one

of the highest in terms of feeling that their job was challenging (88 per cent). It undoubtedly reflects the inherent nature of what is a very demanding job – staff have to work long hours (two-thirds, for example, said they worked, on average more than 10 hours overtime a week), perform a wide range of tasks, and struggle to fill vacancies and absences on the shop floor.

As one store manager remarked:

Section managers have to work bloody hard ... they are more task-oriented than the senior team ... Ideally, section managers should spend 70 to 80 per cent of their time managing, but they do not always do this because of the demands of the job, especially if they have gaps. It's one of the more pressurised roles.

When we look at the correlations (Table 5), we see that there is a positive association between job challenge and job satisfaction and commitment.

This is borne out by the following quote from a section manager:

I believe in the organisation. The grass isn't greener on the far side ... the organisation looks after their staff well although they expect a great deal from people and stretch people ...

In terms of HR practices, the correlations suggest that training and career opportunities are linked to job satisfaction and commitment. This is not surprising, considering that these are first-line managers, most of whom have been promoted from the shop floor, and many of whom were keen to progress further in the organisation. Satisfaction with pay is strongly associated with motivation and commitment, and one possible explanation for this is explored in the following chapter.

Table 5 | The relationship between HR practices and employee attitudes in Tesco – Year 1 correlation results (n = 43)

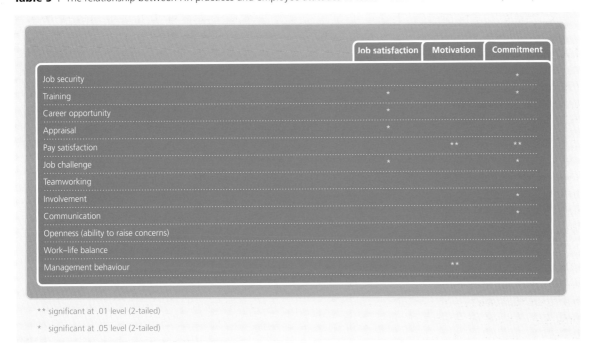

	Job satisfaction	Motivation	Commitment
Job security			*
Training	*		*
Career opportunity	*		
Appraisal	*		
Pay satisfaction		**	**
Job challenge	*		*
Teamworking			
Involvement			*
Communication			*
Openness (ability to raise concerns)			
Work–life balance			
Management behaviour		**	

** significant at .01 level (2-tailed)

* significant at .05 level (2-tailed)

The importance of management behaviour (ie by senior managers and the store manager) is shown in the links to motivation, to commitment in terms of how good these managers are at involving and communicating with section managers, and to job satisfaction in terms of performance appraisal. Although policies and processes are highly routinised in Tesco, store managers and the senior team have significant discretion over how they handle such issues as allowing staff (including section managers) to comment on proposed changes, or respond to suggestions from staff, and in the frequency of performance appraisals. Again, this is examined in more detail in Chapter 3.

AIT[1]

The Big Idea in AIT stems from the beliefs of their founder and current chairman. This is seen not only in the steps the company takes to establish and preserve its organisational culture but also in the way the organisation is structured and in its HR practices.

The organisational culture is very important to the chairman, and is captured by their aim of being,

> **the best organisation
> in the world to work for
> and the best organisation
> in the world to work with.**

Indeed, the Chairman holds strong views about the role of business in society because he does not see a separation between business or work and society. This then produces a particular need to make the workplace a good place to work. Moreover, he believes that it is something of a challenge to make organisations good places to work.

1 The practices and processes described here reflect those in place at the time of the research. However, since that time AIT have undergone substantial changes, although the practices and processes remain intact.

' ... the key criterion for their selection is not their level of technical skills but whether they fit with the organisational culture.'

When asked to sum his philosophy, he suggested it was 'to have fun and make money.'

The fast growth of the organisation, especially in the late 1990s, presented a serious challenge to the ethos and culture of the organisation as the number of employees increased. Indeed, the chairman suggested that:

There is a danger that the culture of the organisation will wash away with a tide of new people.

However, he also commented that:

What survives depends on what you choose to let go of last.

The importance of organisational culture is shown in a variety of ways. In practice, managers seek to apply these principles equally to their customers and to their employees. This was seen as a mutually reinforcing marketing advantage.

In the words of the director of intellectual capital:

It allows us to attract good people who want to work for AIT and provide excellent service for the customer. It is all about forming the right relationships, and these are easily transferred between employees and customers.

This culture is supported in various ways, including a 'visionaire', whose job it is to improve social relations between employees through organising team awaydays, an annual organisation social for all employees, together with a strong social and sporting set of shared activities.

Recruitment and selection assumes central importance in the maintenance of the organisational culture, especially in that much of the entry comprises new graduates. Indeed, the key criterion for their selection is not their level of technical skills but whether they fit with the organisational culture. The local labour market makes it difficult to recruit experienced staff, but there has been a move to employ more of them because of the changing demands of clients. Traditionally, most staff have been recruited straight from university and have a variety of backgrounds; they are then provided with intensive training in the firm. Labour turnover at around 10 per cent is low for the industry

The emphasis on graduates is continued in the training and development programmes. One-third of the budget is devoted to graduate training, which lasts around three months. Training and development for other employees is also important and each employee averages around six days' training per year. However, as with recruitment and selection, this training is not client specific but designed instead to increase the 'stock' of intellectual capital so that AIT is better able to meet and anticipate the needs of a variety of clients and to attract and develop employees they need.

Again in the words of the Chairman:

We want people to be effective when they come to work. We want teams to work together effectively. We want them to be able to communicate well with one another and with the customer. They are more likely to do this if they are happy at work and they socialise with the rest of their team. It is important that these relationships are robust, that they are grown internally so that they can withstand challenges which are placed upon them.

This emphasis on organisational culture is also shown by the organisation's reliance on direct employees, who make up nearly 90 per cent of the staff, rather than the use of large numbers of subcontractors or off-shore working. Teamworking is emphasised, and employees are each usually members of three teams organised around the current project, their profession, and the social organisation of the firm. In addition, there is active management support for extra-mural clubs and societies.

The HR structure itself is well developed and is broken down into human capital (the skills and knowledge of employees), structural capital (the fixed systems in place for collecting, storing and transmitting information – for example, the database and the intranet), and training and development. The HR department controls the allocation of staff on to different projects rather than the operational director, and this allows the function to pay particular attention to the career development needs of employees.

Line managers have a clear responsibility to carry out their HR responsibilities, most importantly the appraisal of their employees, and they are closely monitored to ensure that they are doing this as part of the development of the employees who work for them.

The HR strategy is influenced indirectly not so much by the needs of individual clients as by the conditions within the industry as a whole – which, at the time of the research, were characterised by skill shortages and the fast pace of technical change. More importantly, AIT has a clear HR strategy which is aimed at maximising and developing intellectual capital and playing a key role in managing its relations with its clients. The principal aim here is to develop and retain the skills

– such as non-technical business analysis skills – that are critical to satisfying client needs.

The focus of business activity is on looking forward to try to anticipate client needs rather than simply on managing the present problems or looking back.

The pay and performance management systems also reflect an approach that is not client-specific. The salary structure is not directly affected by clients since it reflects increases in the skill, knowledge and experience of employees. Up to 20 per cent of the activities that contribute to the acquisition of such skill, knowledge and experience can be carried out externally – for example, on community projects. The performance management system rewards performance against project-related objectives, but typically the resulting bonus counts for only around 5 per cent of the total employee reward.

The internal structure of the organisation is built upon a series of communities.

The operational communities are the project teams, which have been developed to work for a particular client. These typically exist for around six months – although some can last much longer – and involve around 12 people including business analysts, software developers, builders and testers.

The vocational communities are effective across these project teams and are made up of specialists such as builders or testers. The groups meet together regularly to discuss issues of common interest across the project teams.

The staff communities are referred to as T-Groups, which are the principal means of internal communication. They are non-hierarchical and cross-functional. The social communities are very strong and include social and sporting teams as well as organisers of the staff awaydays.

There are extensive knowledge-management activities across the organisation, both through the use of formal systems such as an intranet and a document database, and through semi-formal systems which include regular lunchtime briefings and addresses to the whole organisation by the MD. These activities are co-ordinated by the knowledge manager, who is assisted by knowledge mediators whose task it is to stimulate the sharing of knowledge both within and between project teams.

The ability to combine all aspects of human resource and organisational processes together and build a strong value-based organisation was reflected in our interviews with employees. These

comprised a group of young professional software designers in the main. We interviewed 36 in the first year, and 33 in the second year. Job satisfaction was especially high – and much higher than the national average for associated professional employees.

◘ 85 per cent were satisfied with the influence they had over their jobs (WERS 98: 54 per cent)

◘ 61 per cent were satisfied with the sense of achievement they got from their work (WERS 98: 58 per cent).

In the first-year interviews the significant correlations are shown in Table 6.

Thus, for these young professionals, knowing what was going on, having a say in organisational decisions that affected their job or work, working

Table 6 | The relationship between HR practices and employee attitudes in AIT – Year 1 correlation results (n = 36)

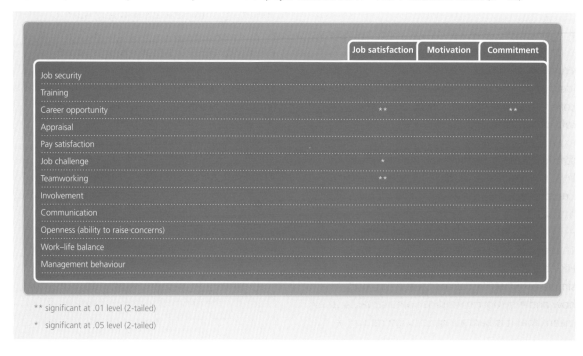

	Job satisfaction	Motivation	Commitment
Job security			
Training			
Career opportunity	**		**
Appraisal			
Pay satisfaction	.		
Job challenge	*		
Teamworking	**		
Involvement			
Communication			
Openness (ability to raise concerns)			
Work–life balance			
Management behaviour			

** significant at .01 level (2-tailed)

* significant at .05 level (2-tailed)

> **' Values and the way the Big Idea is transmitted are important features of the organisational process advantage these firms have.'**

in a supportive team environment, and doing challenging work that helped develop their career skills were all important to them in terms of providing job satisfaction. This is a typical young professional view.

In addition AIT was able to generate high levels of organisational commitment. Particularly important here were the people management skills of managers and the way the organisation tried to create a work–life balance for its staff.

To quote two of our respondents:

It's a good place to work. People generally feel valued – you're not just another number and there's scope for advancement. They encourage you to make more of your skills and abilities.

It's a nice working environment. The most important things are that everyone is helpful and friendly … and competent – there's no blame culture, which you can't take for granted.

Conclusions

We have shown how values – what we call the Big Idea – that are embedded, connected, enduring, collective and measured and managed play a key role in some of our organisations. They help to explain why organisational commitment is so strong, and how individual policy and practices linked to these values are strongly associated with organisational commitment, motivation and job satisfaction.

This, then, is one of the keys to the HR-performance link. It helps us go beyond a simple count of HR policies to begin to understand how and why policies improve performance. It also means that it is hard for other organisations to

copy best practice. It is one thing to design and implement a particular policy. It is quite a different order to create the organisational values necessary for these policies to work effectively. Values and the way the Big Idea is transmitted are important features of the organisational process advantage these firms have.

The sales director at Nationwide often used a metaphor about the need 'to tend the garden'. What he meant was that if you want to harvest the fruit (sales), you need to create the conditions and to grow them. This raises two important issues we explore in the next two chapters.

First, although the important role of line managers is evident already, we need to examine it carefully. This is the next chapter.

Second, 'tending the garden' means that performance for these organisations is about the medium and long term as well as the short. It is about gaining and keeping sustained competitive advantage. In Chapter 4 we look at the HR–performance question not just in the short term but by asking questions about sustainability too.

What is the point of short-term performance if you cannot be fit enough to sustain it and adapt to new challenges?

3 | Bringing policies to life: the critical role of line managers

As noted earlier, in Chapter 1, there is clear evidence that HR policies and practices are a source of competitive advantage. In most large organisations these HR policies are designed by specialists but, crucially, their implementation is in the hands of line managers who are responsible for a group of employees working for them.

In the past decade much has been made of 'returning HR to the line' – but precisely what is being 'returned' is far from clear. Problems of espoused policies not being enacted are quite common, while questions of what priority line managers can give to people management in view of the numerous other demands on their time remains a difficulty. Previous research on people and performance has been largely silent on the role of managers, yet our research sees them as central.

The critical role that all managers – in particular line managers – play in the development and maintenance of employee involvement techniques is, for example, discussed in detail by Marchington (2001). This opens up a much wider area for study which is the focus of this chapter: the ways in which HR policies are put into operation by line managers. In particular we need to examine the exercise of line manager discretion. This is of critical importance for understanding the links between HR policies and business performance, as shown by its central position in the Bath model.

We explore the exercise of managerial discretion by drawing on the work of Fox (1974: 16), who distinguished between two characteristics of work roles.

'Task range' refers to the variety of tasks in a job, which at the one extreme can be highly specific and at the other very diffuse.

The second characteristic is 'discretionary content', which looks at the extent to which the behaviour needed in a job is highly specified or diffuse. More critically, he argued that 'every job contains both prescribed and discretionary elements', and that (Fox, 1974: 19) the discretionary elements

require not trained obedience to specific external control, but the exercise of wisdom, judgement and expertise. The control comes from within: it is in a literal sense, self-control. The occupant of the role must himself [sic] choose, judge, feel, sense, consider, conclude what would be the best thing to do in the circumstances, the way of going about what he is doing.

This is important not just for employees, as we have discussed in the introductory chapter, but also and perhaps especially so for managers, who are more likely to have discretionary elements built into their job.

We argue that the exercise of employee discretion is crucially affected by the way in which managers exercise their own discretion, especially in managing people. Even in the most standardised organisation managers will have some discretion as to how they put HR policies into operation, and employees are more likely to act 'beyond contract' if managers behave in ways which stimulate and encourage this kind of behaviour in their employees. So we are looking not only at employee discretionary behaviour, but also at manager discretionary behaviour – and it is the interplay between these two which is linked to business performance.

For example, the manager who carries out performance appraisal interviews with his or her employees enthusiastically and thoroughly, and who has the leadership skills in communicating

> '... the manager who ... has the leadership skills in communicating and dealing with problems, is likely to encourage employees to reciprocate with behaviour that is similarly "beyond contract".'

and dealing with problems, is likely to encourage employees to reciprocate with behaviour that is similarly 'beyond contract'. Moreover, we argue that it is not only the HR policies which are the source of HR advantage but critically the way that these policies are implemented. This is because although the HR policies can be copied, it is much more difficult to imitate these implementation processes which will be highly specific to the organisation.

Some important parts of these processes are best thought of as practices rather than as policies *per se* since they are about appropriate behaviours like communicating, involving, counselling, guiding, etc. No policy, and no policy manual, can specify how such things are to be done. This is why the issue of values and culture becomes so important in indicating what is deemed to be appropriate and inappropriate managerial behaviour, as discussed in the previous chapter.

Analysing the HR activities of line managers

If we look at the role of line managers in a little more detail, we shall find that the various parts of their jobs are subject to differing levels of discretion. Some aspects of the job may leave virtually no room for choice because the procedures to be followed are tightly drawn and the monitoring of compliance may be very close and frequent. For example, there may be a series of quality checks in a production process which must be followed at all costs. However, there may be other aspects of the job where discretion is much wider. We find that the management of employees is often an area where managers are able to exercise some discretion, or, to put it negatively, are able to ignore some obvious features of good management.

Indeed, one line manager in one of our cases illustrated this point perfectly when she said:

The only area I have discretion over is how I manage my people

– because effectively she had no control over the price, quality, quantity and location of the goods for sale in her department.

In the same organisation a more senior manager referred to those areas over which he had no control as his 'management responsibilities' since these involved activities he was obliged to carry out, whereas he referred to those issues over which he had much more discretion as being his 'leadership responsibilities'. It is these leadership responsibilities that are of particular interest.

It is important to look at the role of managers more systematically if we are to analyse the evidence for and impact of the exercise of their discretion. We have identified four different aspects of the management of people in our model which we believe are important.

Front-line management
– implementing
– enacting
– leading
– controlling

> ' There are a whole series of ... small actions which managers undertake on a daily basis that have a major impact on employees' experience of working life ... '

Implementing HR policies

This refers to whether line managers put HR policies into operation – for example, where there is a performance appraisal procedure, did the line manager actually carry out the appraisals? We are able therefore to compare the responses from employees on whether or not there is a performance appraisal in accordance with the stated policy of the organisation, to see to what extent the reality matches up to that policy. In fact, in all of our case-study organisations that had a stated, formal performance appraisal policy, there were always a number of employees who claimed that they had not been appraised, although the proportion varied between cases. The same sometimes applied in relation to communication activities.

In the Bath model we refer to this as 'implementing'. Here managers are essentially following procedures and taking advice from the HR department and utilising the on-line or published manual to assist them understand what is required.

Enacting

This area is concerned not so much with the extent to which the managers follow or do not follow policy as with the way in which they enact the policy to make it effective. Although a manager may follow the appraisal policy because there is little choice, the manager may do so grudgingly with little enthusiasm or commitment to the process involved.

Here there may be formal evidence of appraisal meetings with appraisal forms appropriately completed, but all of it done in a perfunctory manner and of is little value to either party.

Conversely, other line managers may carry out appraisal enthusiastically and may encourage employees in both explicit and tacit ways. This includes the extent to which managers coach and support their employees and, where appropriate, cultivate a team spirit and undertake the appraisal process. We refer to this as 'enacting' in the model.

Front-line leadership of employees

There are a whole series of, on their own, small actions which managers undertake on a daily basis that have a major impact on employees' experience of working life in their organisations. Many of these test the interpersonal skills of line managers and are concerned with communicating information to employees, responding to their suggestions, treating employees fairly, and managing operational problems. How and when these activities are carried out cannot be captured in a policy handbook. It is as loose as 'good management' – yet value-driven organisations, as described in the previous chapter, are likely to see this as a vital area of the manager's job. They increasingly describe this part of the manager's role as 'leadership'. We use this term in the model.

Controlling employees' work

This is the final area of managers' behaviour concerned with controlling the behaviour of their employees and their influence over the job. It involves a wide range of activities including, for example, the extent to which they closely supervise the work of their employees by checking up on them frequently and monitoring the quality of their work, or alternatively trusting people more to get on with their jobs and allowing them to exercise influence over how the job is done.

The issues here are employee satisfaction with the influence they have over their job, and how employees perceive the way their managers control absenteeism and lateness and manage quality issues. We refer to this as 'controlling' in the model.

Evidence of the importance of the line manager's role

We explore the line manager's role in three ways.

- First, we look across the sample of organisations to find the statistically significant associations with front-line leadership.

- Second, we use data from our second-year interviews in three organisations where significant changes had been made to the front-line managerial role and show how these impacted on employee attitudes.

- Finally, we use multi-site data from Tesco to show how variations in employee attitudes are explained by differences in line management behaviour.

By looking at linear correlations in individual case-study organisations, we are able to explore the links between front-line leadership and satisfaction with other aspects of policy and practice identified in the Bath People and Performance model. We can report only associations and cannot say for certain what is the direction or the nature of the causality, but the strength of the front-line leadership variable is such that the importance of the line manager is clear. By 'front-line leadership' we mean behaviour in managing people on a daily basis using questions evaluating how good managers are at:

- keeping everyone up to date about proposed changes

- providing employees with a chance to comment on changes

- responding to suggestions from employees

- dealing with problems

- treating employees fairly.

When our respondents felt that their managers were good in this type of leadership behaviour, they were also satisfied with a range of other HR policies or practices – particularly those in which line managers play an active role.

The number of strategically significant associations is listed in Table 7 below, as revealed in our organisations using first-year data. The list counts the numbers of organisations (maximum 12) where there were statistically significant associations between satisfaction with front-line leadership and various HR policies and practices.

In other words, in every organisation where employees were satisfied with management leadership, they also felt satisfied with their level of involvement. In nine cases, employees who were satisfied with the degree of involvement they had also showed high levels of organisational commitment. Managers thus play a vital role in making involvement happen, in communicating, in being open to allow employee concerns to be raised and discussed, in allowing people space to influence how they do their job, and in coaching, guiding and recognising performance and providing help for the future. This was clear both for managers in general and the immediate line manager in particular.

Table 7 | The number of significant correlations between satisfaction with front-line leadership and various HR policies and practices (n = 12 organisations)

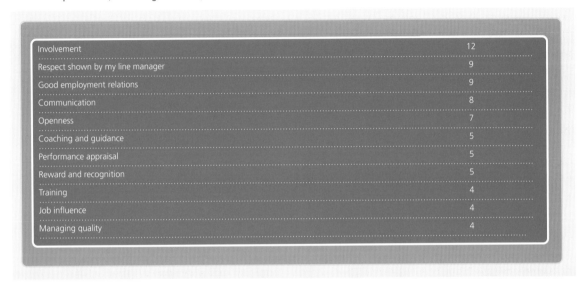

Involvement	12
Respect shown by my line manager	9
Good employment relations	9
Communication	8
Openness	7
Coaching and guidance	5
Performance appraisal	5
Reward and recognition	5
Training	4
Job influence	4
Managing quality	4

Table 8 | Significant correlations between satisfaction with respect shown by immediate line manager and various HR policies and practices in each organisation

AIT	Involvement, leadership, job influence, work–life balance, good employment relations
PWC	Training, job security, teamworking, involvement, job influence, control of quality
Nationwide	Appraisal, involvement, communication, leadership, good employment relations, control over absence/lateness, openness
Clerical Medical	Involvement, leadership, flexibility
Selfridges	Careers, pay, appraisal, involvement, communication, leadership, coaching and guidance, good employment relations, openness
Tesco	Training, careers, pay, appraisal, involvement, communications, leadership, job influence, coaching and guidance, good employment relations, work–life balance
Jaguar	Training, careers, pay, involvement, communication, leadership, job influence, coaching and guidance, control over lateness/absence, work–life balance
OMT	Careers, respect and recognition, involvement, leadership, job influence, coaching and guidance, good employment relations
RUH	Training, appraisal, involvement, communication, leadership, coaching and guidance, sharing knowledge

(NB: No associations were found in Contact 24, Royal Mint, Siemens)

> ' The quality of line management ... clearly matters, as seen through the experience of the employees we interviewed. '

We asked each of our respondents about the extent to which they were satisfied with the respect that they got from their immediate manager, their boss. Those who were satisfied with this level of respect were also highly likely to be satisfied with other aspects of HR policy and practice.

This applied in reverse, too – poor bosses cause dissatisfaction. Looking at the first-year cases, when people were satisfied with the respect their boss showed them, they were also likely to be satisfied with other aspects of HR policy. We show this in Table 8 on a organisation-by-organisation basis, since the patterns are subtly different, indicating the different importance to different areas of HR.

We are not saying in each case that the immediate line manager was the only person delivering these HR policies and practices, but we can say that a person's boss plays an important role. The quality of line management in general, and the leadership capability of a person's boss in particular, clearly matters, as seen through the experience of the employees we interviewed.

The significance of this is discussed later, in Chapter 5, where we show that dissatisfaction with existing policies is a more powerful influence on attitudes than the absence of policies.

Improving front-line leadership

Having compared front-line leadership across all the case-study organisations, we now focus on changes over time in three organisations.

The Royal United Hospital, Bath

We studied a clinical unit in the hospital. This had moved to a new, purpose-built site just before we did our first-year interviews. At that time these revealed a command-and-control approach to ward management which was not appreciated by those we interviewed.

However, marked changes in employee attitudes took place between Year 1 and Year 2, mainly in response to some clear changes in people management practices and policies. This was despite the fact that the hospital experienced exceptional difficulties and was being branded with a very poor reputation nationally. At ward level, for example, deliberate efforts were made to improve management by careful selection, emphasising leadership skills beyond just medical competence, by providing support and training to front-line managers and by introducing a new 360-degree appraisal system which the manager would have to manage.

The results are shown in Table 9. This table shows the percentage who were satisfied. (A more accurate picture is revealed by the mean scores, and these are shown in Appendix 2.)

It is clear that the changes made in the hospital were recognised by the staff, most of whom were nurses. There was a marked increase in satisfaction over the amount of influence people had in their jobs – satisfaction which rose from 45 per cent to 62 per cent. It was the changes in satisfaction with line management itself that was most impressive – 89 per cent of our respondents now reported that they were satisfied or very satisfied with the respect they got from their line manager, and almost half felt that managers were good at dealing with problems in the workplace, compared with a third in the previous year. In the same vein the number of employees who felt that managers were fair rose from a third to two-thirds, and the overall perception of the state of employee relations rose from 21 per cent to 51 per cent.

' **Difficulties with retention and filling vacancies is a major problem for the NHS generally.** '

Table 9 | Employee satisfaction with aspects of HR policy and practice: RUH
Percentage of respondents who said they were 'very satisfied' or 'satisfied'

	Year 1	Year 2
Policy practice	%	%
Job influence	45	62
Appraisal	55	74
Sense of teamworking ('very' or 'fairly strong')	82	91
Work–life balance ('good' or 'quite good')	29	41
Management		
Manager good at responding to suggestions	29	37
Manager good at dealing with problems	36	49
Respect shown by the line manager	66	89
Outcomes		
Job satisfaction	79	83
Motivation ('very' or 'fairly' motivated)	79	94
Commitment (share the values)	38	57
n =	42	39

Many respondents recognised that this was due to the change in their immediate line manager.

We have a new manager who is very approachable – a good listener who gets to learn a lot ... People go to her ... She's very supportive. In six months the atmosphere is totally different in a good way.

Communication on the ward is excellent now. Our manager is very approachable. She's in the coffee room with us, and so on.

[on appraisal] It's useful to know what my peers think of me ... and my line manager has the right skills for feedback.

This improvement was not evident in those facets of people management outside the control of the line manager. Thus satisfaction with pay increased only slightly (30 per cent compared with 24 per

cent) and benefits stayed virtually the same (84 per cent to 83 per cent). Indeed, when looking at attitudes towards the Trust as a whole, there were reductions in feelings of involvement (16 per cent satisfied, compared with 24 per cent) and involvement in future plans (roughly a half compared with two-thirds previously).

We can therefore see clear evidence of the impact of the arrival of the new ward manager, but we can also see the limits of her influence, especially where attitudes were affected more by Trust decisions than by local leadership at the ward level.

To the senior manager in charge of the department the acid test was the impact on vacancies. Difficulties with retention and filling vacancies is a major problem for the NHS generally. In Year 1 this was certainly the case in this ward, where 11 out of 32 posts were vacant. However, in the second year, after the changes, there were no vacancies at the time we finished our interviews.

Selfridges

There was a very similar pattern in Selfridges, where changes associated with the role of the first line manager/team leader seem to have been influential. Despite numerous changes nationally – including the opening of a new store in Manchester – at local level in Trafford Park, where we did our research, action was taken to try to reinforce certain aspects of HR policy and practice following our first-year interviews. In particular, action was taken to improve how team leaders undertook 'front-line leadership'. Team leaders had to re-apply for their jobs – with the consequent departure of some of them – and there were improvements made to the performance appraisal scheme, such as linking the scheme to succession planning, and thus working more on career opportunities.

As noted earlier (see Chapter 2), these were topics identified in the first-year survey results as areas of possible weaknesses given the very high expectations engendered by the 'value from values' statement.

The outcome, seen in the second-year results, was impressive. This was true both when we compared the matched sample of people interviewed in each year and when we compared those who were interviewed for the first time in Year 2 with the Year 1 sample. Table 10 shows the percentage who were satisfied. (The mean scores for a selected series of questions are shown in Appendix 2).

These changes coincided with an improved perception of the role played by line managers/team leaders. For example, there was an increase in the perceived respect from the immediate line manager (from 88 per cent to 92 per cent), in the view of how good managers were at responding to suggestions (43 per cent to 59 per cent) and at

Table 10 | Employee satisfaction with aspects of HR policy and practice: Selfridges
Percentage of respondents who said they were 'very satisfied' or 'satisfied'

	Year 1	Year 2
	%	%
Appraisal	59	84
Career opportunities	70	88
Manager good at responding to suggestions	43	59
Respect shown by the line manager	88	92
Job influence	68	73
Job satisfaction	68	83
Motivation ('very' or 'fairly' motivated)	93	92
Commitment ('I feel loyal to Selfridges')	81	93
n =	40	41

providing everyone with a chance to comment (25 per cent to 34 per cent). These changes might be explained by the greater emphasis on the team leader role.

There were also improvements in employee attitudes towards some HR policies. For instance, in Year 1, 70 per cent of staff were satisfied with their career opportunities, while by Year 2 this had reached 88 per cent. Similarly, the proportion of those who were satisfied with their method of performance appraisal rose from 59 per cent to 84 per cent. These are quite large changes in a relatively short period of time, and are probably accounted for by changes to the team leader role and the appraisal scheme – as the following quote from a sales associate suggests:

We now have a manager who gets the appraisal done … and we get praise now and little gifts, such as perfume …

In Year 1 the responses for employee pride, loyalty and sharing organisation values were already quite high, but by Year 2 there have been increases especially in those who *strongly* agreed that they felt loyal to the organisation (17 per cent to 39 per cent), shared the organisation's values (3 per cent to 15 per cent) and who felt pride when telling people who they worked for (29 per cent to 48 per cent).

Both of these cases show how organisations can focus developmental policies on the role of line managers and how these consequentially have a beneficial effect on the staff that they manage. What happened in the RUH and in Selfridges was not simply luck in making good appointments but was the outcome of careful planning and forethought by the HR teams in each organisation.

Clerical Medical

A very similar pattern of results was evident in Clerical Medical, where a new manager in charge of one part of our unit of analysis wanted to bring in more team-based involvement, improve the operation of the appraisal system and generally improve brand awareness and efficiency. This was as part of the organisation initiative called 'Living the Brand' which included 'succeeding through people' and 'people first'.

Learning and Development Agreements were introduced, and new starters had 'learning pathways'. Involvement was focused on off-the-job projects for small groups of staff.

On the whole, the outcome was positive. The comment from a department manager who had been active in introducing the change was:

Some managers did not like it, and team leaders were surprised because it had not been done before.

During our two surveys a lot of changes also took place at team leader and management level, partly driven by expansion in some areas and reductions in others. Teams were smaller, and greater emphasis was placed on the team leader role in people management issues. 360-degree feedback was also introduced for all department managers and team leaders.

Job satisfaction, motivation and commitment all improved. For example,

◧ 88 per cent felt satisfied with the influence they had over their job in Year 2, compared to 67 per cent in Year 1

' **Employees who suffer poor levels of satisfaction and motivation in general may well be transferring their feelings over to specific HR practices.'**

- 70 per cent felt proud to tell people who they worked for in the first year, increasing to 85 per cent in the second year.

The following quotes are from employees who felt more satisfied with their jobs.

I have a new boss who lets me get on with my job. I'm trusted again.

I'm included in more stuff than before, such as people management work and work with team leaders. There's more variety.

In particular, people's satisfaction with management leadership increased substantially – 65 per cent, for example, felt managers were good at responding to suggestions in Year 2, compared with just 41 per cent in Year 1. The same applied to appraisal, teamworking and communications where line managers were particularly influential. The following quote illustrates this point:

It's improved here over the last twelve months – in communicating, managers are more approachable now and aware of what staff feel …

These three case studies clearly show the influence of managerial discretion. We now turn our analysis to look at differences between sites within the same organisation.

Multi-site comparisons: Tesco

We researched in four Tesco stores. Each was in a market town and demographic, labour market and income patterns in these towns were generally similar. Tesco is a centralised, highly successful retail giant with clear routines and policies emanating from Head Office, designed to guide management behaviour at store level.

We should expect there to be a low level of variation in the exercise of managerial discretion in this environment at store level, but in practice there were significant differences. These variations seem to be about the way in which senior managers at store level were exercising their discretion when putting Head Office routines into operation. This is a particularly important area of discretionary behaviour since, as one store manager in Tesco explained,

The routines should be viewed as providing a focus and structure … They are necessary in terms of delivering best practice – but it is the way in which the rules and routines are implemented that makes them effective and brings them to life.

Table 11 shows distinct differences between the four stores in each area of the line manager's role: enactment, controlling and leadership. Levels of job satisfaction, motivation and commitment are shown at the base of the table. It is clear that Store C in particular is out of line with the others. How can we explain this?

Enacting HR policies

Perhaps most intriguing of all is that this pattern of satisfaction and commitment is also reflected in terms of attitudes towards certain HR practices in Tesco, as shown in the table. Both Stores A and C have low scores for satisfaction with levels of training, opportunities for career advancement and satisfaction with the appraisal system. Variations in the levels of satisfaction with pay are especially interesting, given that the pay rates for these employees are standardised across all four stores – yet as few as 9 per cent of employees in Store C are either satisfied or highly satisfied with their pay, compared with 64 per cent in Store B.

Table 11 | Employee satisfaction with aspects of HR policy and practice: Tesco
Four stores compared – Percentage of respondents who said they were 'very satisfied' or 'satisfied' (n = 43)

	Store A	Store B	Store C	Store D
HR policies	%	%	%	%
Training	46	82	36	90
Career opportunities	64	91	55	70
Pay	46	64	9	60
Appraisal	50	82	64	90
Controlling				
Influence over how job is done (% a lot)	64	64	27	50
Job influence	82	82	36	100
Sharing knowledge (% good)	64	82	18	70
Leadership (% good)				
Chance to comment on changes	53	72	18	30
Respond to suggestions	27	82	18	60
Deal with problems	73	82	55	70
Treat employees fairly	64	100	64	70
Provide coaching/guidance (% a lot)	46	55	27	40
Respect shown by the line manager	100	91	64	90
Outcomes				
Job satisfaction	64	73	64	80
Motivation (% 'very' & 'fairly' motivated)	55	46	36	40
Commitment (% proud to tell people who I work for)	91	73	46	90

Employees who suffer poor levels of satisfaction and motivation in general may well be transferring their feelings over to specific HR practices. This has profound implications for the focus on HR policies in providing the necessary environment for discretionary effort since perceptions on and satisfaction with these policies is clearly influenced by the context in which they are applied.

Controlling

The table also shows variations along the controlling dimensions of discretion. There are, for example, marked differences between the stores on the extent to which employees claim they have influence over their job. 27 per cent of employees in Store C say they have a lot of influence over their job, compared to 64 per cent who say this in Stores A and B, and 50 per cent who say this in Store D.

Only around one-third of employees in Store C are satisfied with the level of influence they have over their jobs and 18 per cent are dissatisfied. This compares ill with the other stores, especially Store D where all the employees are satisfied with the level of influence over their jobs.

These two measures are likely to be highly influenced by the way local managers implement the rules and job descriptions set by Head Office. This applies too to sharing knowledge, Store C being particularly poor.

However, there are fewer variations in the extent to which employees find their jobs challenging, perhaps because this reflects the inherent nature of what is basically a very demanding job which is less susceptible to local interpretation in terms of what has to be done – but the local interpretation is how the job can be done.

Leadership

The table shows that there is a high level of variation in employees' perception of the exercise of managerial discretion in the way line managers carry out their jobs in people management terms, what we call leadership. Employees in Store C consistently have a poor perception of the way their senior managers exercise their discretion; the responses in this store are either the lowest or the equal lowest across all of the measures.

This suggests that senior managers in Store C had, at the time of our interviews, a very controlling style of managing which is considered poor in terms of, for example, allowing staff to comment on changes and responding to suggestions from employees. This compares to around three-quarters of employees in Store B who think their managers are good at these things. The relatively poor results for Store C were repeated, but in a less noticeable way, when their results were compared with others in terms of how good managers were at dealing with problems in the workplace, treating employees fairly and showing respect. The other distinct pattern was the consistently good performance of Store B across all the measures.

The impact of local store managers is clear to see here. Even though there is a heavy standardisation of routines, local senior managers are able to exercise their discretion in how they put these into practice, and this is clearly reflected in employee perceptions. The following quotes from our interviews reflect this:

It's a good organisation to work for but the management within individual stores varies and … in terms of their style of management – there are different styles in different stores.
(Section manager)

Store managers have to interpret what Head Office wants … and there is a lot of room for discretion. Effectively the store manager is the interface between the Head Office and those who work in the store. The key is how you apply the Head Office policies – that's very different.
(Store manager)

Getting the right managers into the right store is the biggest issue I have to deal with. (Regional director)

Conclusion

Our analysis has highlighted a number of important findings.

First, we have demonstrated that there are clear variations in the way policies are brought to life within the organisation and how this can change over time. This appears to be related to the interplay between managerial and employee discretion.

Second, variations in employee attitudes towards their job appear to 'spill over' to their attitudes towards HR policies in the round. This says something about the climate of employment relations and the culture and values an organisation lives, since these impact more broadly across all policy areas, and it is here that the role of line managers becomes central. We have seen how deliberate action to strengthen the line management position in the RUH, in Selfridges and in Clerical Medical had substantial beneficial effects. The implication is that this is a clear area where policy can be targeted with beneficial outcomes.

Interestingly, our study has parallels with research undertaken in Canadian banks conducted by Bartel (2000). She concluded (Bartel, 2000: 20) that site managers

create a human resource management environment that can impact on site performance.

In particular, in her study in a bank, it was the quality of the performance feedback system and the quality of communications between the manager and the staff that had significant effects on site performance (ibid: 28). The last word comes from an interview with a department manager at Clerical Medical.

Interviewer: 'What HR policies do you find most helpful?'

(thoughtful silence)

Manager: *'It is the quality of team leaders that is important. If they take a close interest in people and processes, it makes a big difference. You can see this comparing my two teams.'*

4 | The HR–performance link

Introduction

There has always been a strong intuitive feeling that the way people are managed affects business performance, but it is only since the mid-1990s that the research has been available to support this view. Studies by authors such as Mark Huselid and Jeffrey Pfeffer and many others have provided clear-cut evidence of the link between HR practices and the performance of the business (see Boxall and Purcell, 2003, for a more detailed discussion of this evidence).

This data, together with renewed attention paid to the resource-based view of strategy, has given increased credence to the view that HR policies and practices can be a source of competitive advantage. However, as we noted briefly in Chapter 1, there are problems with establishing this link between people and performance.

Problems when linking HR practices and performance

Surprisingly few organisations, including many of the relatively sophisticated organisations we studied, have tried to prove the people–performance link on a regular basis. This and other problems have limited our ability to conduct the kinds of analysis that we would have wished.

Perhaps the most basic problem of all was that the relevant data was often not available. In some cases the data – for example, on the extent of use of HR policies, employee attitudes and performance (aside from financial performance) – simply did not exist.

Some of our organisations did not collect employee attitudinal data, while their performance data was largely designed for internal and external accounting purposes or was not available in any detail for our unit of analysis.

In others, the problem was having too much rather than too little data. In some instances – for example, Jaguar – there were multiple measures of performance with frequent collection of the relevant data. The difficulty here is picking out the key measures and interpreting the data when it is providing conflicting signals.

This is linked to the issue of who 'owns' the data. Quite often, each functional area collects its own data and may be required to report on key measures (typically, in HR, labour turnover, vacancies and absence), but these different types of measures are not co-ordinated, and when they are, they can show conflicting patterns. This in turn raises organisational political issues: whose data is more important, and who is responsible for taking remedial action?

Some of our organisations – for example, Nationwide, PWC, Tesco, Siemens and Selfridges – seek to solve the problem of performance measurement by employing a balanced scorecard approach which is designed to ensure that performance is measured broadly to take account of the factors that are critical to the success of the business. This involves looking not just at financial performance but also at the views of other stakeholders such as customers and employees.

However, problems remain because the setting of targets themselves is a political process which often involves a process of negotiation and takes account of previous performance. Similarly, the importance given to different criteria will be influenced by functional perspectives and individual bias.

> ' ... the period over which performance is measured
> is important. Our organisations vary greatly in how
> frequently they measure performance ... '

Even if these problems can be solved, difficulties remain with making the link between people and performance. In many instances managers are acutely aware of the other factors that affect performance, so that 'like-for-like' comparisons are fraught. There may be changes in technology or market fluctuations, which can make comparisons between periods difficult. In knowledge-intensive organisations such as AIT it is very difficult to establish a link between inputs such as knowledge sharing and outputs such as contracts for new business won, because many of the processes involved are tacit and not easily identified.

Finally, the period over which performance is measured is important. Our organisations vary greatly in how frequently they measure performance, ranging from hourly monitoring of takings in Tesco to quarterly reviews in AIT. More important is the period during which the link between people and performance is studied. It may be relatively easy to produce a short-term improvement in performance lasting two to three months, but the key question is: how robust is this change?

Most organisations are looking for sustained improvements in competitive advantage rather than a short-term fix which then fizzles out. Moreover, the performance measures used sometimes changed over the period studied, making year-on-year comparisons difficult.

We noted in the first chapter that 'performance' is never enough. There is a need for organisations to be flexible to cope with future needs. This has been well observed in studies of lean organisations (Hutchinson et al, 1998). It may be possible to cut costs significantly, but this may impair the capacity of the firm to innovate and meet new challenges: leanness becomes organisational anorexia.

Our approach

As we have noted, our research design tries to overcome some of the problems identified in three ways.

First, we have used measures of performance that are most relevant for each organisation. Indeed, in each case we have taken advice from the senior managers involved in this activity. Trying to establish the same measures in each organisation is simply not feasible although, where possible, we have tried to use common basic measures – for example, labour turnover[1] and absenteeism. In many instances we use operational rather than financial criteria because even at the level of the unit of analysis there are a number of factors that affect financial performance. This approach follows that of some of the most interesting earlier research (eg Arthur, 1994) which used operational data in tightly defined units of analysis.

Second, we have sought to minimise the gap between the level at which performance data and employee data is collected. Thus we have collected performance data, where possible, for the unit of analysis rather than for the organisation as a whole, and as far as possible we have tried to match this to the evidence collected on employee attitudes and the relevant HR policies. For each unit of analysis, we have chosen operational targets which are important to it and which are likely to be directly related to its business strategy.

It is these targets or measures that are likely to be really important, and be ones where employee discretion is likely to have a measurable impact. Examples here may be quality or wastage rate or levels of customer satisfaction. Pure financial

---

[1] Even labour turnover is fraught with problems as a measure since it is influenced by the state of the external labour market and by internal changes. Rumours of downsizing can lower turnover if people think there is a chance of redundancy compensation – and when it happens, by definition, turnover goes up. The measures of labour turnover used also vary: some organisations include for example redundancies, others do not.

measures of the sort reported publicly for the whole corporation are much more remote, and numerous other factors cloud the relationship between input and output.

In short, we need to find measures that are meaningful to the firm and that are likely to be susceptible to employee behaviours. If we can answer these questions, we can then begin to look more closely at the intricate links between HR practices and business performance.

Finally, we have taken care to collect data over the period of the study, in most cases around two years and sometimes longer. We are able, therefore, to compare performance between the two years of data collection. As we have said, the key question for most organisations is not can they make a short-term gain, but can any advantage they have be sustained over the longer term, and crucially, how and why is this advantage sustained?

It must be admitted, however, that two years is still a short period. Ideally, measures would be over a five-year period at least in order to get trend data. One reason for this is the problem of lag. How long does it take for an HR initiative to feed through into measurable outcomes? It is not unusual to find people suggesting a three-year lag for the full effects of a complex change initiative to be seen.

Linking people and performance

Before we look at our data, we have to return briefly to the model we have been using throughout this report. We have made some progress in this area by establishing that a gap exists between espoused and operational policies

which can be attributed to the exercise of discretionary behaviour by managers. This in turn has an impact on the discretionary behaviour of employees, which we believe is critical to performance. We now need to investigate this in more detail.

We shall now look at the data on the links between people and performance in some of our cases in two ways. First, two of our cases are multi-site organisations and collected data in a way that was suitable for our analysis. This allowed us to make comparisons across the organisation at the same point in time. In other organisations this cross-sectional data was not available, and we consequently looked at changes over time.

Tesco

In the previous chapter we showed how employee attitudes were markedly different in the four stores we studied. One store in particular – Store C – was experiencing difficulties. Can we show connections with performance?

Table 12 shows that a variety of measures have been used, although most of these are operational because they most closely reflect the actual performance of each store. These measures are:

- availability – stock availability on the shelves

- known loss – wastage

- shrinkage – unknown loss resulting from theft and stock errors

- one in front – a measure of how often the store achieves its set target of one or fewer customers in the queue at the checkout

□ payroll costs as a percentage of sales

□ profit contribution

□ turnover (£million).

It is clear from the data that Store C was the poorest performer in a number of key areas. For example, its expenses were 28 per cent higher than the average and its profit contribution was 34 per cent lower. It seemed particularly poor at managing wastage, which was one of the key indicators used by Tesco. In contrast, Store B had expenses which were 2.4 per cent lower than average and profits which were 21 per cent higher. Store A had profits which were 13 per cent below the regional mean and Store D had profits which are almost at the mean. Other measures of performance also followed this pattern in which Stores B and D were generally above-average performers and Stores A and C were below average, the performance of Store C being particularly poor.

These performance measures are among a group of the key indicators used by Tesco on their 'steering wheel' to assess operational efficiency, and they link these to their business strategy and financial success.

The findings from Tesco are clear. Even though it is a highly standardised organisation seeking consistency in all its practices, we have evidence – noted in the previous chapter – of variations in the implementation of HR practices and of employee views of the ways managers exercise their discretion.

Stores A and C were generally lowest in terms of managerial behaviour, employee discretion, employee attitudes and overall performance, compared with Stores B and D. There was a strong association between employee attitudes on a wide variety of job design and HR practices, employee views on the quality of HR management applied to them, especially the opportunity to participate, and store performance.

Table 12 | Tesco Performance Data Year 1: Percentage variation from regional average (20 stores)

	Store A	Store B	Store C	Store D
Availability	−0.1	0.6	−0.8	0.3
Waste/known loss	−5.5	4.7	−11.8	7.1
Shrinkage/unknown loss	5.4	63.5	−59.5	44.6
Operating expenses as percentage of sales	2.4	2.4	−28.2	−11.7
Waiting to be served	2.4	−6.9	−0.6	−3.3
Payroll costs as percentage of sales	−4.3	14.8	4.3	0.1
Profit contribution	−13.0	21.4	−33.7	−0.1
TURNOVER £m	42.6	71.1	48.2	54.8

Note: We used actual data to compute the variation from the regional average, and report here the percentage differences for the average of all stores in the region. A minus indicates below-average performance and a positive figure is above-average performance.

' ... the ways in which store managers exercised their discretion affected the willingness of employees to go 'beyond contract' and consequently to improve or sustain business performance.'

It was possible to trace a pattern of results that were repeated through the different kinds of data which linked the exercise of discretion, employee attitudes and store performance. Indeed, we argue that the ways in which store managers exercised their discretion affected the willingness of employees to go 'beyond contract' and consequently to improve or sustain business performance. Given the location of the stores in four similar market towns, and the application of common policies, the most credible explanation for the variation in store performance was the difference in the way people are managed.

As we have described, the employees interviewed were section managers who had some freedom over how they carried out their jobs, particularly in the people management area. We suggest that the way section managers exercise this discretion is particularly affected by the many ways store managers undertake their leadership responsibilities. The section managers meet the store manager frequently, and these meetings can be intense if there is a short-term operational problem to be solved virtually immediately. Not only is interaction frequent and intense but store managers have a high degree of freedom over how they handle issues such as allowing employees to comment on proposed changes, responding to suggestions for change and providing coaching and guidance, as well as how they implement HR practices such as conducting appraisals.

Store managers thus have considerable choice over how they manage their people, within standardised routines, and this in turn affects the way section managers exercise their discretion, which is also mostly over people management issues.

The store manager is particularly influential in setting the tone for the way of managing employees across the store. He or she provides a role model through his or her own way of managing the staff and sets the expectations for achieving certain goals and behaviours that are acceptable when dealing with individual employees. It is possible that the power of the store manager is unusual and a characteristic of ways of managing within the retail sector. Certainly this can be contrasted with Nationwide, where the influence of a single manager is not so important.

Nationwide

It will be recalled that there were 40 or so FCs within the region which formed our unit of analysis. Each of these FCs was a member of one of eight teams (reduced to seven in Year 2) under the control of a senior financial consultant (SFC). However, the FCs met their SFC only relatively infrequently – perhaps once or twice a month – but came into much more frequent contact with the members of staff in the branch, including the branch manager, where they were based.

There are many measures of performance which might be used in this organisation, including the number and value of sales, the value of bonus earnings or various measures of performance on either an individual or team basis. We have chosen to use a measure of individual efficiency – the ratio between the number of presentations made to clients and the number of products sold – because this is less likely to be influenced by demographic factors such as the characteristics of the population in the local area. Using this data, we have explored the associations which exist between employee attitudes towards HR policies and practices and their individual measure of efficiency compared with the mean score. This is shown in Table 13.

Table 13 | Nationwide Performance Data: the ratio between presentations to sales for financial consultants – second year (n = 49)

	Performance ratio	Percentage variance from the mean in performance
How satisfied are you with the amount of influence you have over your job?		
Satisfied	203.4	2.01
Neither satisfied nor dissatisfied	185.1	−7.17
Dissatisfied	184.3	−7.57
Mean (all)	199.4	
Change in satisfaction over the past year		
More	204	2.77
Same	199.6	0.55
Less	187	−5.79
Mean (all)	198.5	
Change in level of motivation over the past year		
More	207.2	4.59
Same	197.3	−0.4
Less	184	−7.12
Mean (All)	198.1	
Managers good at responding to suggestions?		
Good	197.1	−1.15
Neither good nor poor	203.4	2.01
Poor	189.7	−4.86
Mean (all)	199.4	
Managers good at dealing with problems?		
Good	200	0.30
Neither good nor poor	207.7	4.16
Poor	190.7	−4.36
Mean (all)	199.4	
Managers good at treating employees fairly?		
Good	200.6	0.60
Neither good nor poor	191.3	−4.06
Mean (all)	199.4	

> ' **Working with our 12 organisations over**
> **a period ... it was clear ... that the one**
> **certainty was change.'**

Using this data we identified two types of associations with HR policies and practices.

First, there were employee attitudes towards HR practices – shown in the top part of the table – which were positively associated with improved performance and led to a competitive advantage. Put more simply, improvements in these employee attitudes were associated with higher-level performers. These were a high level of satisfaction with influence over the job, and improvements in job satisfaction and motivation.

Second, there were those attitudes and practices that were associated only with reductions in performance. Their presence did not seem to generate improvements in performance. The absence of these attitudes seemed thus to generate a negative effect, but their presence did not have a positive effect. The best that could be hoped for was a 'non-negative effect', because in many ways the FCs took these practices for granted. These key practices were line managers responding to suggestions, dealing fairly with employees and solving day-to-day problems. If FCs had not carried out these aspects of their role well they would effectively be creating a source of competitive disadvantage.

Tesco and Nationwide were multi-site operations, allowing us to make comparisons between sites. Elsewhere, we were comparing changes in performance between two years.

Improving and sustaining performance over time

Working with our 12 organisations over a period of 24 months, and some cases 30 months, it was

clear – sometimes painfully so – that the one certainty was change. The twin requirements discussed in the first chapter of 'fit' and 'flexibility' were much in evidence. That is the continued need for HR to fit with or be appropriate for the business strategy, delivering high performance, while simultaneously being flexible enough to help adapt to new circumstances or contribute to the achievement of successful change.

There are two types of situation we wish to discuss in this section. First, there are organisations that we know have made changes to their HR practices between the two years of data collection, and we are keen to study the impact of these changes. Second, there are those organisations that have not made such big changes but that have experienced significant changes in external competitive environment which have potentially placed the link between people and performance under strain; here the key task is to sustain performance.

We showed in the previous chapter how three of our organisations had made significant improvements in employee attitudes between the first and second years of our study.

We noted how in the RUH the staff vacancies for nurses dropped significantly, and for the senior manager responsible for our unit of analysis, this was, to her, the most important measure. It was immediate and meaningful, and it was managing staff retention that she found crucial for improved patient care. It was not possible to collect other data here, in part a reflection of the problems the hospital was experiencing at senior management level.

> ' **The power of HR polices and practices to influence performance is always limited by extreme circumstances.'**

In Clerical Medical, performance continued to improve with market share in the critical Independent Financial Adviser (IFA) market rising. Labour turnover remained at the same rate as in the previous period (14.5 per cent).

Selfridges have a battery of performance measures covering finance, productivity, staff and customer satisfaction. Overall, in the period at the end of our study compared to the previous year, sales were up 23 per cent, payroll costs down 5 per cent, and 'contribution' – the key measure of sales against payroll costs – up 31.7 per cent. In our main unit of analysis, ladies' wear, where we know changes took place, they had the best record of labour turnover and the second lowest absence rate (4.9 per cent). All the indicators were pointing in the same direction of success.

We are not able to say, and nor is anyone else, what part improved people management made to this achievement, but given the centrality of people management to the Selfridges' story of regeneration, no one doubts its significance. It is not thought necessary to prove the precise contribution, in relative terms, of HR to this collective endeavour. What measures they do use soon show up problems when they occur. This is the logic of the balanced scorecard approach as it looks across a range of measures for early indications of difficulties, rather than focusing only on the outcomes of profit or shareholder value.

These cases indicate a clear association between people management and performance in the context of changes made to HR policy and practice.

There are three other organisations in which the changes in the external environment were more significant and posed a significant challenge for managers seeking to maintain employee attitudes and sustain, if not improve, performance.

The Royal Mint provides an example of an organisation which found it very difficult to sustain employee attitudes, and demonstrates a link between people and performance in the reverse direction to that seen so far – falling profitability and declining staff attitudes.

The Mint ran into difficulties as the boom in re-coinage following the introduction of the Euro in Europe and new currencies elsewhere such as Hong Kong, was not replaced with new orders, and the price per tonne for export orders collapsed by £300 to £400 per tonne. The Mint reported its first loss for many years in the period between our first and second year interviews, and a round of redundancies was announced. The long-term security of working in the Mint, set up in the high-unemployment black spots of the Welsh valleys in the early 1970s was shattered (just 20 per cent felt their job was secure in Year 2 compared to 50 per cent in Year 1).

The outcome in this case was much in line with predictions, and it is hard to imagine what other possibility there could have been. The power of HR policies and practices to influence performance is always limited by extreme circumstances. Here there were dramatic falls in job satisfaction, motivation and commitment, and people perceptions of management behaviour in terms of communication and responding to suggestions fell too.

For example, just under half (46 per cent) felt satisfied with the sense of achievement they got from their work in Year 2, compared to three-quarters in Year 1; 81 per cent felt proud to tell people who they worked for in Year 1, falling to 57 per cent in Year 2.

Two of our other cases, Nationwide and AIT, told a different story. Indeed, Nationwide is one of the most interesting cases to study over time because this organisation has faced changes in its market position during the period of the research. There was increased competition for business, pressure to reduce costs and a change in the key mortgage proposition of the Society. These changes could potentially have had a big influence on employee attitudes and behaviour, especially in our unit of analysis, as the FCs found themselves under more pressure to deliver.

A number of competitor organisations withdrew from direct sales while others cut back. Within Nationwide a decision to withdraw from the discounted mortgage market led to a predicted loss of branch referrals (ie leads) to financial consultants. A restructuring programme took place involving changes to the basis for bonus payments and the way in which the FCs' performance was appraised. This reduced pay for many, sometimes substantially. There was more of a requirement to be team players and to focus on their personal development and their approach to work, rather than just meeting individual sales targets. There was an expectation at the time we undertook the second round of interviews, in the autumn of 2001, that attitude changes would reflect these difficulties and commitment to the Nationwide would have fallen significantly. We might have expected to see reductions in job satisfaction and commitment and more pressure being placed on the relationship between the SFCs and the FCs.

Attitudes did change towards particular features of HR policy and practice, but the fundamentals remained remarkably stable, as shown in Table 14. (A more accurate picture is revealed by the mean scores, shown in Appendix 2).

It was hardly surprising to find that pay satisfaction was down, as was satisfaction with the appraisal process since this contributed to pay and more

Table 14 | Nationwide employee attitude survey data Year 1 and Year 2
Figures show the percentage 'satisfied' or 'very satisfied'

	Year 1	Year 2
Job security	87	74
Job influence	89	78
Job satisfaction	84	78
Motivation ('very' or 'fairly' motivated)	96	92
Pay	93	86
Managers good at responding to suggestions	77	69
Managers good at dealing with problems at workplace	75	71
Respect from the line manager	91	92
Commitment – pride	93	86
– loyalty	89	92
– share the values	96	98
n =	44	49

stretching targets were being set. FCs were less happy with the amount of influence they felt they had over how they did their job. Job satisfaction fell.

Satisfaction with managerial behaviour fell slightly, while measures on the respect shown by the FCs' immediate boss remained stable. This was at a time when we might have expected there to be pressure on the line manager–employee relationship.

What is particularly interesting in this case with understandable reductions in job satisfaction was the way in which both motivation and commitment held up at the very high levels revealed in the first year. There was even an

increase in commitment levels, which remained among the highest of the 12 organisations in the study. This may be indicative of the underlying values of 'mutuality' as lived within the organisation (discussed more fully in Chapter 2).

Looking at the statistical correlation between aspects of policy/practice in this second, difficult year and organisation commitment (Table 15), it is clear that managers have continued to put effort into applying these policies and practices, especially those we summarise as front-line leadership, as described in the previous chapter.

The real test of any system of HR is when the organisation faces difficulties and hard choices have to be made; when communication is about

Table 15 | The relationship between employee evaluations of HR policies and practices and organisation commitment – Nationwide correlations for Years 1 and 2

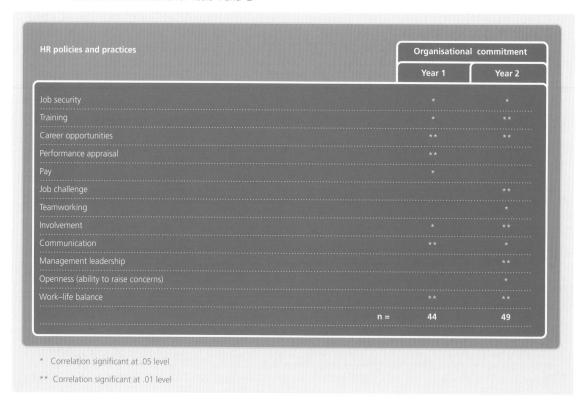

HR policies and practices	Organisational commitment	
	Year 1	Year 2
Job security	*	*
Training	*	**
Career opportunities	**	**
Performance appraisal	**	
Pay	*	
Job challenge		**
Teamworking		*
Involvement	*	**
Communication	**	*
Management leadership		**
Openness (ability to raise concerns)		*
Work–life balance	**	**
n =	44	49

* Correlation significant at .05 level

** Correlation significant at .01 level

' **The real test of any system of HR is when the organisation faces difficulties and hard choices have to be made ... '**

bad news, not success; when work is being intensified, earnings drop and some jobs are lost. Here, the Nationwide came through remarkably well. The Group HR director's view is that strong, consistent values are essential and provide the platform for achieving change and taking difficult decisions. The results here seem to bear him out.

Overall in Nationwide we have seen a remarkable degree of stability in employee attitudes and behaviour at a time when we might have expected marked reductions.

AIT virtually collapsed in 2002, suffering a catastrophic drop in its share price because of problems with reporting its financial results, which led the organisation to move to the alternative investment market. This was after we had finished our second round of interviews, but even then there were indications of some difficulties – elements of job satisfaction were falling as the organisation tried to develop a new range of products based not on a bespoke service to clients but on licensed software requiring up-front investment.

However, the very strong values noted earlier as part of the AIT Big Idea remained dominant. With the gathering storm, people's loyalty to AIT increased – 85 per cent reported feeling loyal to the organisation in Year 2 compared with 61 per cent in Year 1. This is a measure of affective commitment: people wanted to stay working for AIT. Even though the labour market was not quite so buoyant as it had been there were still plenty of jobs available for the highly skilled professionals of AIT. If AIT had been unable to keep its staff in really difficult times, as a knowledge-based organisation it would have collapsed.

Conclusion

Our study has demonstrated convincingly that research which asks only about the number and extent of HR practices can never be sufficient to understand the link between HR practices and business performance. As we have noted, it is misleading to assume that simply because HR policies are present they will be implemented as intended.

Despite the carefully standardised practices of the four Tesco stores we have seen marked variations in the way they are operated and in employee responses to, and perceptions of, these practices. These variations are also reflected in the variations in performance in each store. Similarly, we cannot assume that all HR policies and practices will have a positive effect on performance.

In Nationwide, when looking at the association between HR practices and various changes in performance, we found that some, when effectively managed, had positive associations, while others that were less well managed had negative outcomes. Studying changes over time, especially where there are clear changes of policy, makes it easier to pick out the people–performance link.

In the RUH, Selfridges and Clerical Medical the success in people management were all reflected in improvements to performance.

However, in many ways the key issue was the robustness of these associations between HR policies and business performance, and the extent to which competitive advantage could be sustained. We argue that those organisations with

> ' ... those organisations with the Big Idea that were values-led and managed were much more able to sustain their performance over the long term.'

the Big Idea that were values-led and managed were much more able to sustain their performance over the long term. It means that not only are the HR policies themselves important but that the way they are put into operation also contributes to the HR advantage. This is shown particularly well by the Nationwide and AIT cases.

There are, of course, a variety of possible explanations for this pattern over and above those we have discussed. For example, as mentioned in the introduction to the report, in Tesco there might be a 'halo' or 'horns' effect as described by Wright and Gardener (2000) whereby employees who for example work in a high-performing store will have a more positive view of their discretion. In other words, the direction of causation goes from performance to attitudes via discretionary behaviour, rather than from attitudes to performance. A feedback loop is therefore included in our Bath People and Performance model in Figure 1 (Chapter 1).

A key conclusion is the need to keep this sense of success going, and the 'halo' effect of positive feedback can help sustain performance during the tougher times. This is where powerful underlying values that are embedded are so important. We have sought to capture this by including a feedback loop in the Bath model.

5 | The effects of HR policies

Previous chapters have looked in detail at key themes: the role of values as the bedrock of policy effectiveness, the crucial role of line managers in bringing policies to life and in practising good people management, and the way these link into performance. We draw some general policy conclusions in the next chapter while noting that every organisation is different. We can, however, explore policy implications in a different way through the use of our employee questionnaire in these 12 firms, repeated in the second year, and in the six organisations covered in the sister project on knowledge-intensive firms (Stuart *et al* 2003).

This unique database is large enough to allow us to look for deeper statistical associations with the aim of identifying what matters to employees: what HR policies and practices impact on commitment, motivation and job satisfaction? We use each of the 11 particular policies identified in the Bath People and Performance model and see to what extent they are influential.

So in this chapter we use the whole database to identify the way in which employee perceptions of the effectiveness of policies impacts on their motivation, job satisfaction and organisational commitment. Given the size of the database we are then able to see if there are differences between the experience and attitudes of the three occupational groups. We look at team leaders or junior managers, professionals, and workers.

In that our aim was to look very broadly at the full range of issues associated with people management, our questionnaire covered a very wide range of issues. This range has both advantages and disadvantages. On the plus side we are able to explore a large number of issues – far wider than previous research, much of which

has tended to list policies to test their existence. The disadvantage of this breadth of analysis is that we were forced to use only one or two questions in each area. For example, we used only one question to explore motivation, one for job satisfaction, and three for organisational commitment. This limits how far we can predict a precise link between policy and employee response.[1]

We use a particular statistical technique (ordered probit) that allows us to explore the full range of responses to the questions on levels of motivation, commitment and job satisfaction. (For example, job satisfaction was graded on a 5-point scale ranging from 'strongly agree' to 'strongly disagree'.) Multivariate analysis of this sort means that we can identify the power of each variable individually and in combination with others.

In this way we go a long way towards revealing the drivers of motivation, commitment and satisfaction. Here we report our initial analysis. There is much more that will be done later in refining this approach. We are able to use a number of control variables such as age, gender, and tenure with the organisation and in the job. Most valuably we use the wide range of factors explored in the questionnaire to look at the connections with motivation, job satisfaction and organisational commitment. These factors are shown in the checklist below.

Checklist of questionnaire factors

- ◘ job security

- ◘ job influence

- ◘ job challenge

1 Psychologists who focus exclusively on the concept of motivation would use up to 10 questions to explore this one construct.

- career opportunities

- training and development

- pay satisfaction

- links between pay and performance

- stress (worry about work at home)

- work–life balance

- appraisal

- involvement

- teamworking

- openness (ability to voice concerns)

- management leadership

- coaching by line managers

- communication

- management efficiency in dealing with quality, lateness and absence

- respect shown to employees by their line manager

- the state of employee relations in the firm.

The determinants of motivation, job satisfaction and commitment

Motivation

Using the 4-point scale (not at all motivated, not very motivated, quite motivated, and very

motivated), just over half of our sample of 1,000+ said they were 'quite motivated', 27.5 per cent said they were 'very motivated', 14 per cent claimed to be 'not very motivated', and a tiny number (37 people in all) felt they were not at all motivated.

The determinants of motivation are multiple. Not surprisingly, given the high degree of overlap between motivation, organisational commitment and job satisfaction (Cronbach's alpha of 0.77), motivated people were highly likely to have satisfying jobs and feel committed to their firm.

Key policy/practice issues that influence levels of motivation

- job influence

- career opportunities

- job challenge

- involvement in management decisions

- training

- line manager respect.

We can be more precise about this by using a benchmark analysis for the 'ideal' employee. This benchmark, or baseline, employee who is our point of reference corresponds to a person who is satisfied with each of the policies and practices outlined in our questionnaire checklist (above). We then explore how much less likely this benchmark individual is to be highly motivated if he or she is not satisfied with one of these policy-practice areas. This analysis enables us to show the importance or the value of each of these policies in influencing motivation.

Figure 4 | The effect of dissatisfaction with given policies and practices on motivation
Percentage decline (n = 1,037)

Source: P&P and KIFS questionnaire

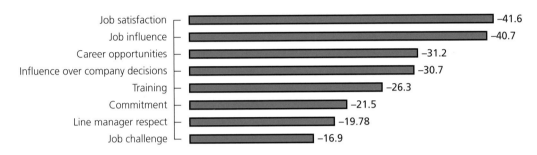

The results are shown in Figure 4, which lists those practices that have an effect. Other policies, not listed, are neutral in their influence.

So if, for example, we take an individual who is identical in all respects to the 'ideal' employee except in relation to career opportunities (in other words, that person is dissatisfied with career opportunities), this person will be 31.2 per cent less likely to be motivated than the 'ideal' person.

Job satisfaction

Using the same type of benchmark or baseline analysis of the 'ideal' employee we can see the key drivers of job satisfaction. This is shown in Figure 5. The survey question addressing job satisfaction was 'How satisfied are you with the sense of

achievement you get from your work?' Just over half of our respondents were 'satisfied', 18 per cent were 'very satisfied', a further 18 per cent were 'neither satisfied nor dissatisfied', just under 1 per cent were dissatisfied, and 20 people were very dissatisfied.

Key policy/practice issues that influence levels of job satisfaction

◘ job influence

◘ career opportunities

◘ job challenge

◘ teamworking.

Figure 5 | The effect of dissatisfaction with given policies and practices on job satisfaction
Percentage decline (n = 1,037)

Source: P&P and KIFS questionnaire

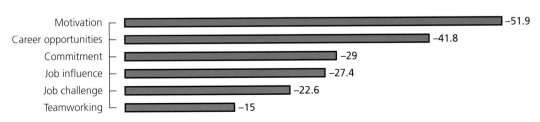

Organisational commitment

We apply the same type of baseline analysis again to organisational commitment. We measure organisational commitment as a combination of three questions from our survey. These questions asked the respondents to express their level of agreement/disagreement with the following three statements:

- ◘ I feel proud to tell people who I work for.

- ◘ I feel loyal to [organisation name].

- ◘ I share the values of [organisation name].

These answers were coded on a 5-point scale from 'strongly disagree' up to 'strongly agree'. Summing these values creates a 13-point scale ranging from zero (strongly disagree with all three statements) to 12 (strongly agree with all three statements).[2]

For computational and presentational ease we separate workers into three types based on their responses. Very committed workers (27.2 per cent) are those who score at or above 10 on our scale.

This means that these employees have answered 'strongly agree' to at least one of the constituent questions. The uncommitted workers (13.5 per cent) are those who score at or below 6. A person who answered 'neither agree nor disagree' to all three questions would fall into this category. The other employees (40.7 per cent) lie between these extremes.

Key policy/practice issues that influence levels of commitment

- ◘ training

- ◘ career opportunities

- ◘ job challenge

- ◘ management leadership

- ◘ performance appraisal

- ◘ work–life balance

- ◘ communication on organisational performance

Figure 6 | The effect of dissatisfaction with given policies and practices on organisation commitment
Percentage decline (n = 1,037)

Source: P&P and KIFS questionnaire

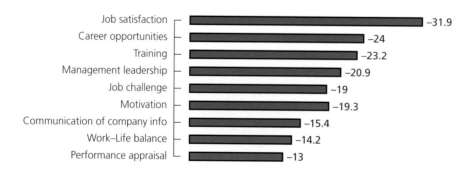

[2] Cronbach's alpha for the construct consisting of these three questions is 0.75, and as such we believe the combination of these variables into a single construct is reasonable.

> ' Other factors ... especially influential ... are the
> sorts of policies and practices that go into
> making a firm a great place to work ... '

Figure 6 uses the same benchmark, baseline analysis of the 'ideal' employee to analyse the effect of poor policy and practice in reducing commitment.

A number of common factors emerge as influential from inspection of Figures 4, 5 and 6. Opportunities for career advancement influences all three attitudinal areas, while job challenge, job influence and training feature in two areas.

Interestingly, there was a strong link between those who said their job required them to work very hard and those who reported that their job was challenging. And those who worried about their work outside working time were also much more likely to have high levels of commitment to their organisation.

Other factors were especially influential in impacting on organisation commitment. These are the sorts of policies and practices that go into making a firm a great place to work, as opposed to influencing an individual's job. They included involvement, the respect received from the boss, teamworking, management leadership, the openness of the firm, efforts to help achieve work–life balance and communication.

Differences between occupational groups

In the course of the research we aimed to interview front-line staff whether on the factory floor, in the office, in call centres or serving customers. This range has enabled us to divide our respondents into three groups. It became clear that different occupations respond to policies and practices in different ways.

Team leaders or junior managers are people with some leadership responsibilities but often are not formally recognised as being on the managerial ladder. Typically, they are in between non-managerial staff and appointed managers above them. For example, in Jaguar they were group leaders, in the RUH ward sisters, in Tesco section managers. There were 240 such people in the sample.

Professional staff are those who would normally require some externally certified education or training to get and keep their jobs – people in our sample like accountants, software engineers, nurses, mechanical engineers. There were 340 of these.

Workers are those who are neither team leaders/ managers nor professionals. For want of a better word we call these 'workers', whether they are on the factory floor, are sales associates in retail stores, are customer service associates in call centres, or are porters in hospitals. There were 457 of these.

Team leaders/junior managers

Using the same analytical method of a baseline standard of the team leader/junior manager who is exposed to good policy/practice produces some interesting results. Here, for brevity's sake, we report on the most important two or three variables predicted to influence levels of attitude, but we go further in showing the effect of policy/ practice combination. This is particularly useful since it is rarely the case that only one policy/ practice is floundering while all the others are fully effective. Analytically it is useful to show the power of each variable, but examining combinations of factors illustrates the way these policies cumulate. For team leaders the key factors reducing motivation, commitment and satisfaction are shown in Table 16.

For example, a person who is dissatisfied with his or her training or who has not received training will be 63 per cent less likely to be committed than our 'ideal' employee.

We can surmise that training and career opportunities are particularly important because these team leaders/junior managers want the possibility of doing better now and in the future. They want to work in an organisation where their immediate boss treats them seriously (with respect) and where they can express their opinions.

Let us give an illustration from one of our manufacturing organisations, all of which used team leaders extensively. Team leaders were the crucial channel of communication both downwards and upwards. Where their team members made a suggestion or raised a problem it was the team leader who communicated this upwards to the supervisor (or whatever the job title of the next level of manager was). If the more senior manager, the supervisor, treated this matter seriously and the team leader was able to report back on action taken, his or her job became much more satisfying and worthwhile. If the supervisor was dismissive, the demotivating effect was noticeable.

There was a widespread desire for training in both the technical aspects of the job and in 'soft' leadership skills – for example, team-briefing and problem-solving. Given that nearly all of them had been promoted to team leader/junior manager, they not unnaturally had career aspirations and wanted career opportunities. Table 16 shows what happens when these hopes and aspirations were not met.

Professionals

The cliché is that managing professionals is like herding cats. Most professionals have the capacity to be relatively mobile, so commitment to the (current) organisation can be harder to achieve than job satisfaction and motivation. We reported on these tensions in our recent report on knowledge-intensive firms (Swart et al, 2003).

It is often harder to gain organisational commitment from professionals than from other occupations because they can often build their

Table 16 | Key policy/practice factors that influence team leaders'/junior managers' levels of motivation, commitment and job satisfaction

HR policies and practices	Motivation	Commitment	Job satisfaction
Dissatisfaction with, or lack of :	%	%	%
– respect shown by the manager	−50.5		
– job satisfaction	−49.5	−27.2	
– career opportunity	−37.8		−56.1
– training		−63.0	−60.3
– openness		−55.9	
Combined effects of policies in column	−96.0	−98.4	−90.3

' ... **organisational features like job design, opportunity for advancement and involvement or voice mechanisms [are] key HR policy and practice areas which impact on worker attitudes ... '**

career by moving around, and their job – their 'craft' – is the dominant feature of their work. While the likelihood of job satisfaction drops steeply when people do not feel they have career opportunities, it was organisational commitment that was most susceptible to policy/practice failure. For example, the likelihood of commitment to the organisation fell by:

◘ 35.7 per cent where managers had poor leadership skills

◘ 38.1 per cent where the job was not challenging

◘ 22.1 per cent where not enough attention was given by the organisation to work–life balance

◘ 36.4 per cent where pay was not related to performance

◘ 25.7 per cent where there was judged to be a poor climate of management–employee relations.

Professionals with low levels of job satisfaction, with poor managers and with no pay–performance link had a combined loss in the likelihood of organisational commitment of 93.6 per cent. This is important because retention is vital, and organisational commitment is the most obvious factor outside pay satisfaction which influences this. It happens because professionals who think they are managed badly by their bosses in leadership terms (eg problem-solving, keeping people up to date, responding to suggestions, etc) are less likely to be committed to the organisation – but they are more likely to be satisfied with their jobs ('We don't need managers around here!').

Workers

This was our largest occupational group and covers a wide range of people in our varied organisations. Generally, in line with other surveys, the workers' levels of motivation, commitment and job satisfaction were lower than for professionals and front-line leaders. The key factors affecting the three attitudinal components are shown in Table 17.

Table 17 | Key policy/practice factors that influence levels of motivation, commitment and job satisfaction among workers (non-managerial, non-professional employees)

HR policies and practices	Motivation	Commitment	Job satisfaction
Dissatisfaction with or lack of :	%	%	%
– career opportunities	–46.2	–35.8	–48.9
– influence over job	–63.7		–57.2
– involvement in management decisions	–36.6		
– job security		–41.2	
– job challenge			–46.4
– job satisfaction		–58.5	
Combined effect of policies in column	–96.3	–93.3	–93.2

The data here may not be surprising since it shows that workers in dead-end jobs (no career) which are simple (not demanding), where job methods cannot be changed (no job influence), and where managers do not allow employees to have a say in decisions which affect them, will be demotivated, uncommitted and dissatisfied employees.

Put positively, the policy implications point to organisational features like job design, opportunity for advancement and involvement or voice mechanisms as key HR policy and practice areas which impact on worker attitudes and their willingness to engage in discretionary, useful work behaviour.

Conclusion

In this analysis we have used a benchmark of the 'ideal' employee exposed to best policy and practice to show the effect that the lack of a particular policy or practice has on levels of motivation, job satisfaction and commitment. The proportion of employees who are exposed to every one of these policies and practices is, of course, a minority. Even if these policies are applied, they might not operate in a manner that is satisfactory to the employee.

A third of our front line leaders were highly motivated, just under a fifth were satisfied with their jobs, and a third had very high levels of commitment to their firm. Roughly similar results were found with professional employees, although they were more likely to be highly satisfied with their jobs than other groups. The lowest proportion of highly motivated, committed and job-satisfied employees were workers. Only 23 per cent were highly motivated, 20 per cent were committed, and 15 per cent gained high levels of job satisfaction.

One way to look at this is to suggest that a lot of improvements could be made and, given the connection with discretionary behaviour, this would be likely to improve performance. Our detailed analysis of the top organisations in our sample of 12 suggests that this is probable. However, the cost benefit analysis of improvements in these employee attitudes is rather more complex. Not every employee 'wants' or is willing to 'give' high levels of commitment, and implementing yet more policies may not change this position.

Our analysis shows that dissatisfaction with existing policies is a more powerful influence on attitudes than the absence of policies when it comes to organisation commitment – at least in the organisations we were studying, which already had a higher number of HR policies than average. Where employees were dissatisfied with existing policies, satisfaction fell by 38.8 per cent from the baseline level of full satisfaction. Where the policies did not exist, and people were dissatisfied with this, commitment fell by 16.9 per cent.[3] Yet again, policy application or enactment comes through as a major issue. Developing yet more policies may be a waste of resources: getting existing policies to work better will be likely to pay dividends in increasing organisational commitment. This is especially the case in terms of career opportunities, job design, involvement and line manager leadership skills.

---

3 In the case of job satisfaction there was no difference, while for motivation, dissatisfaction with the lack of policy is more important than dissatisfaction with existing policies.

6 | The implications for HR policy and practice

This wide-ranging study of the impact of people management on business performance, undertaken over 30 months in 12 organisations, has raised a host of important issues in people management. These are:

1 Managing performance through people means finding ways to induce or encourage employees to work better or more effectively by triggering the discretionary behaviour that is required, to a great or lesser extent, in order to do a job well. This happens when people find their jobs satisfying, they feel motivated and they are committed to their employer in the sense of wishing to stay working for the organisation in the foreseeable future. It is the role of HR policies and practices to build this connection to discretionary behaviour by providing policies and practices which make work, and the working environment, satisfying and motivating.

2 Particularly important policies and practices which came through in our statistical analysis and seen in our case studies are:

  – opportunities for career advancement

  – doing a challenging job

  – having some influence on how the job is done

  – opportunities for training

  – having a say in decisions that affect the job

  – working in teams

  – working for a firm that assists people to balance home and work

  – being able to raise matters of concern

  – having a boss who shows respect

  – having managers who are good at leadership.

3 For team leaders/junior managers, the relationship with their boss and the openness of the firm in that matters of concern could be talked about were particularly important in addition to career opportunities and training. For professionals, job challenge and linking pay to performance were key attributes, with management leadership and work–life balance also important. Workers were particularly concerned to have secure, good jobs, career opportunities and a sense of involvement.

4 The most successful organisations with higher than average levels of organisational commitment were those with a clear vision and a set of integrated values. They had what we call a Big Idea. These values were embedded, connected, enduring, collective and measured and managed. This meant the firms also were likely to use a balanced scorecard or equivalent to show the interconnection between operational, financial, customer-related and people dimensions of management, both in the sense of measuring for early indicators of problems and as a means of integrating decision processes.

5 The most successful organisations were concerned to sustain performance and find a

' ... getting existing policies to work better is more
likely to pay dividends in terms of increasing
commitment than developing new policies.'

means to be flexible. This means the HR policies and practices must 'fit' with or be appropriate for the business strategy, while at the same time being flexible enough to help organisations adapt to changing circumstances. Enduring values played an important part in achieving this.

6 In some cases, lower levels of commitment were explained more by dissatisfaction with the way in which policies and practices were implemented and put into action, rather than by the lack of a given policy. In other words, getting existing policies to work better is more likely to pay dividends in terms of increasing commitment than developing new policies.

7 Implementing and enacting policies is the task of line managers. The way they exercise leadership in the sense of communicating, solving problems, listening to suggestions, asking people's opinions, coaching and guiding, and controlling lateness, absence and quality makes the vital difference. Organisations that did this better in the second year showed marked improvements in employee attitudes, and in performance.

8 Proving that HR contributes to performance is not a major issue, and measures which use profit or shareholder values are too remote from the practice of people management to be useful. What is important is operational measurement where a close link can be observed, and the regular collection of these measures covering people, operational, financial and customer areas is commonly done in the best firms, linking back to the logic of the balanced scorecard.

9 There is clear evidence of a link between positive attitudes towards HR policies and practices, levels of satisfaction, motivation and commitment, and operational performance. Furthermore, there is some evidence to suggest that negative employee attitudes towards the job affect attitudes towards HR policies. For example, employees suffering from poor levels of satisfaction and motivation may well transfer their negative feelings over to specific HR practices.

Here we briefly look at the policy implications of these findings.

The policy-practice mix

We have gone a long way beyond the counting of HR policies usually found in earlier research, and can assert that policy and practice implementation is the vital ingredient in linking people management to business performance. What seems to be happening is that successful firms are able to meet people's needs both for a good job and to work in 'a great place'. They create good work and a conducive working environment. In this way they become 'an employer of choice'. People will want to work there because their individual needs are met – for a good job with prospects linked with training, appraisal and working with a good boss who listens and gives some autonomy but helps with coaching and guidance. But, in addition, the firm in general is a great place to work. Teamworking is positive, managers are effective and open, there is good communication and a sense of involvement, and relations between management and employees are good. This twin requirement to meet individual aspirations and be a great place to work is not easy to achieve. In our judgement, Nationwide and Selfridges were able to do this. Others were good

> '**Two longstanding features of people management remain vitally important in influencing employee attitudes ... careers and training.**'

at one aspect or the other, while a few were unable to meet either.

Values: the Big Idea and the role of HR

The policy implications of this are clear. Organisations wanting to maximise the contribution that people management makes need to develop policy and practices which seek both to meet the needs of individuals and to create a great place to work. Beyond that, as we noted in Chapter 2, there is a need for values and culture which bind the organisation together, which give it focus and which can be measured and managed. We call this the Big Idea, since it is related to what the organisation stands for and what it is trying to achieve. This points to the need for unified action, values and purpose from the top management team, not just the HR department. It is not something that can be done overnight, and indeed it is one of the secrets of successful organisations, since it concerns organisational process advantage and is extremely difficult to copy. It has to be created uniquely in every organisation and takes time, vision and energy.

It was also evident in the organisations that had successfully adopted this approach over a number of years, that HR management was fully integrated into the management process, and understood the interconnection between customer satisfaction and employee attitudes and behaviour. They were themselves embedded into the organisation not as a stand-alone function but as integral members of the management team. Their contribution was valued.

Policy focus

Looking at individual policy and practice both within each of our organisations and across the whole of the data (which show employee *perceptions* of policies and practices), some key policy implications can be drawn.

- Two long-standing features of people management remain vitally important in influencing employee attitudes and helping to create positive discretionary behaviour. These are *careers* and *training*. This is not the place to debate the so-called end of careers, or whether self-directed training is better than formal training courses. What our data shows is that the employees have expectations of something beyond just doing the job. Zella King (2003) has recently shown how graduates have career aspirations and expect their firms to meet them. This does not mean a career for life in the same firm, and what people mean by a career is probably different now from what it was a generation ago. Our data shows this wish for a career – or what loosely could be called a developing future – is true for most people. Training is valued because it holds the promise of learning to do things better, or doing new things. It is the sense of progression and purpose that is important, especially in linking to organisation commitment.

- *Job design* is an area that deeply influences people's experience of work. It is clear that where people have some influence over how they do their job, and where they find their job demanding and challenging, they are much more likely to have job satisfaction, be motivated and be more committed to the organisation in the sense of wanting to stay – affective commitment, as it is called. There is nothing new in this finding, and the fact that this confirms most earlier research on the importance of job design adds weight to the evidence. However, there was little sign that

> ' ... for a firm to be viable it will need a basic number
> of policies and practices ... What makes a difference is
> how these policies and practices are implemented.'

management think seriously about this. Too often job design is taken for granted and presumed to come out of technology. This is not true. All jobs are socially constructed. This is an area where HR professionals could play a much more important role – for example, by being members of project teams designing new workplaces and work processes using insights on the vital importance of job challenge and job influence.

- Another old chestnut is *involvement* and *communication*. The opportunity to contribute to decisions and have a sense of involvement is valued by most people and was linked to organisational commitment. Where managers encouraged involvement, this was associated with satisfaction with management leadership. This is again something that we have known for a long time, but the evidence here is clear and reinforces the central message that designing and managing involvement and communication systems are a major part of successful HR policy and practice, and one which is deeply influenced by, and involves, line managers. Involvement is not just a matter of policy. Our evidence is also clear that the perceived freedom to raise concerns and grievances – what we call organisational openness – is also highly valued. The common term frequently used these days to cover involvement and openness is 'voice systems'.

- *Appraisal* is valued. Interestingly, all three of the organisations which made significant change and improvement between the two years of our study have revised their appraisal process to broaden both those involved (eg 360-degree in the RUH) and the scope of the discussion, making it more developmental. This had positive outcomes. Professional staff also

wanted to see a link between performance and pay, but this is never easy to achieve.

- *Work–life balance* came through as another important topic influencing employee attitudes and connecting these with positive employee attitudes. Work–life balance had different meanings in different organisations. For example, for professional employees, especially those on project work, it often meant a recognition by the firm of the need to manage the issue of work demands that conflicted with home life. In some of the manufacturing plants, where there was less of an issue of long working hours, it was more to do with the way in which the firm shows practical compassion helping people deal with family trauma. This was one of the areas commonly included in people's perception of their firm as a great place to work.

Line managers

It is relatively easy for firms to copy particular HR policies, so the existence of a policy mix is not a source of competitive advantage. Indeed, within a given sector of the economy for a firm to be viable it will need a basic number of policies and practices, what are called 'table stakes'. What makes a difference is how these policies and practices are implemented. This is where the role of line managers in people management is crucial.

Time and again in our case studies, whether interviewing senior executives or employees, the way line managers implement and enact policies, show leadership in dealing with employees and in exercising control came through as a major issue, and was often something of a concern. We explored this at length in Chapter 3.

It was also very clear when we did the statistical tests on our sample of interviews. This showed both that the respect the employee gets from his or her immediate boss is linked to positive attitudes in terms of commitment, motivation and job satisfaction, and that it is also linked to the perceived effectiveness of other policies and practices such as job influence, coaching and guidance, and communication. More generally, what we call 'front-line leadership' – keeping everyone up to date, providing a chance to comment, responding to suggestions, dealing with problems, being fair – was widely recognised by employees and was linked to positive outcomes. We have reported on the three organisations that focused on this area, and each showed marked improvements in employee attitudes. Front-line leadership matters.

In all the debate about leadership in organisations, attention is usually focused at the top where mission, values and the Big Idea come from. This is, of course, important as we have shown. But our research also shows unequivocally that it is the delivery of these values, and associated policies and practices, by front-line managers and team leaders that really counts.

They have to have the policies to implement and the time to engage in leadership and control, as well as enacting the HR policies. They also need training and support.

It is not just about getting good managers but about establishing the context in which they can be good managers, and providing them with the policy tools to do the job well. When we looked in Chapter 5 at our sub-group of team leaders and junior managers, by far the most important factor influencing their motivation was the respect they were shown by their boss, while the big influence

on organisational commitment was the openness of the organisation – how easy it was for them to raise grievances and matters of personal concern.

This draws attention to the type of relationship front-line managers themselves have with their bosses up the hierarchy. More generally, our research points to the need for particular HR policies and practices to be designed for, focused on, front-line managers, and on building a middle and upper tier that supports them since this is where the people management sources of competitive advantage spring from when linked to values.

Performance

Most of the managers we talked to in our organisations did not go out of their way to prove that people management influences business performance. They knew that already and were, in any case, sceptical of the type of measures used in the past to show the link with profit or share value. For them, there was too big a gap between policy in HR and the ultimate measures of profit and 'too much noise' (ie other variables) in the system to know exactly how HR had an effect in a measurable way. In any case, circumstances always changed so that it was hard to compare like with like.

What was of concern were operational measures covering employees, customers, cost efficiency, revenue, and the way these were interconnected, or could be.

It is important to recognise what these measures were used for. They were not used to prove the value of HR or justify the existence of the function. In most of our organisations HR was mature enough, and respected enough, not to need this,

' **Our research has helped some ...
firms already.'**

although they always wanted to understand how the link is made between people and performance. Our research has helped some of these firms already. Internal organisation measures and data were considered to be highly important as a means of identifying problems and monitoring progress and as a guide to policy innovation. Some were used as leading indicators helping to predict downstream profit and performance. Leading indicators were always more difficult to collect and interpret, but usually of more value.

The use of the balanced scorecard or the 'tomorrow's organisation' model of 5 + 1 did help where the focus was less on the pure measures and more on the processes of decision-making and decision analysis, and where these were linked to values and the Big Idea. It is important to recognise the political nature of performance measurement as an inevitable feature of organisational life. For this reason, and for clarity and focus, a few key measures owned by more than one function are better than lots of measures. Then the debate, and the politics, are over interpretation and subsequent action can be more focused and fruitful. We frequently found that where there were lots of measures in use they had an unfortunate habit of pointing in different directions at once, such that no clear message emerged and each function championed its own data sources.

None of our organisations, as far as we were aware, had found a way of measuring change and flexibility. AIT did try to get measures of innovation since this was a key business activity, but not of flexibility, adaptability or change. Yet these 'flexibilities' were the very attributes which were most valued highly and were seen to link directly to the ability of the organisation to sustain performance in different business circumstances.

Change and flexibility are essentially intangible qualities, the building blocks for continuous high performance which cannot be effectively measured yet are recognised as key attributes of long-run successful firms. It is in this intangible area where good people management, broadly defined, was especially important in helping to sustain performance in good times and bad.

Appendix 1:

The research design

The key features of the research design were:

1   We identified organisations that were either known for the quality of their human resource management or were actively seeking to improve the link between people management and performance. Of the 20 or so organisations that were initially approached, 12 eventually agreed to co-operate with the research. (A short profile of the case-study organisations is provided as an Annexe to this Appendix.) A further organisation dropped out of the research when a major merger and reorganisation restricted research access. We are very grateful to all these organisations, their managers and employees for their co-operation over a two- or three-year period and for their active involvement in the Advisory Council which met regularly to assess the progress of the research and to help in the identification of the key themes and ideas. A distinctive feature of the research was working in partnership with these organisations. The 12 organisations, the unit of analysis and the number of employees interviewed in Year 1 is shown in Table 1 (Chapter 1). Each of these organisations had a large number of HR policies and practices. In David Guest's survey (2001), also funded by the CIPD, where he counted the number of HR practices that organisations were using, only a small minority had 11 or more practices out of a total number of 18. In our survey, which deliberately focused on sophisticated organisations, one had eight policies, two had 10 policies and the remainder had more than 11, five of them having 15 or more policies which covered a majority of employees. This meant that we were able to concentrate on the effectiveness of policies linked with performance, rather than be concerned simply with the number of policies each organisation had.

2   In each case we chose a unit of analysis as the focus for the case study. This is shown in Table 1 in Chapter 1. A unit was an identifiable area within the bigger business organisation which was small enough for us to be able to identify a sample of employees to be selected for interview, and where this number of employees would constitute a reasonable proportion of the total number. This was also a unit where performance data would ideally be collected in order to attempt to show a direct connection between people and performance.

3   In each case we used a detailed questionnaire in our face-to-face interviews with employees. These employees were normally front-line staff, or direct production workers with a minimum of one year's service. We repeated these interviews a year or so later (with the exception of Siemens Medical where only first-year interviews were conducted). Where possible, we interviewed the same people in the second year, but given labour turnover, shift patterns and absence this was never complete. We therefore filled our quota by interviewing new respondents. On average, each interview lasted 50 minutes. The first-year interviews were conducted in the period July 2000 to September 2001, and the second-year, where possible, one year later. The purpose of the face-to-face interviews, rather than using a self-completion questionnaire, was to ensure both a high response rate (it was very rare to have a refusal to co-operate) and to enable us to explore understandings and explanations of why each person gave a particular answer to various attitudinal questions. This allowed us to collect a large number of verbatim quotations and find out why people felt motivated, had organisational commitment or found their job satisfying, and helped us to understand why they thought certain aspects of the

organisation's HR policies were positive or negative. This is a unique feature of our research allowing for both qualitative and quantitative analysis.

4   Some of the questions in the questionnaire were taken directly from the employee survey in the 1998 Workplace Employee Relations Survey (WERS 98). This allowed for comparisons and benchmarking both nationally and by occupation and sector.

5   Elite interviews were conducted with senior management to understand how the business operated at site or unit level and, in each case where unions played an active part, also with local union leaders. Line managers responsible for the unit of analysis were interviewed using a semi-structured questionnaire designed to explore how people management practices and policies were managed and implemented on a day-to-day basis in their area.

6   In the élite interviews with policy makers our concern was to understand the history and current circumstances of the business environment and its effect on HR policy and practice. We also wished to explore, in detail, questions of organisational values and culture, and the way these influenced HR and performance. These interviews allowed us to identify the key contextual variables and the historical path taken by each organisation.

7   Our approach to performance data was to ask the organisations to identify the performance measures they considered the most important and where the link with people management was most likely to be observed. Our justification for looking at this level of data is that HR is primarily an operational activity and

we wished to identify the direct connection between people and performance. We sought to do this by collecting the performance in the unit of analysis and not at the firm level. We wished to explore the direct connection between the employee views, the line manager responses and performance within the unit. Even this proved very hard to achieve because in many cases the performance data was not available. This is explored in Chapter 4.

8   We fed back the results of the first round of research to each of the participating organisations, and to most in the second round. Our research thus took on attributes of action research where the research influences subsequent policy. In a number of cases – notably the RUH, Clerical Medical, Selfridges and Tesco – we were aware of action taken following the first-year research feedback and were able to monitor its effects in the second round. This is described in Chapter 4.

9   In 2001 the CIPD commissioned us to undertake a linked research project on people management and performance in what were then Growing Knowledge Intensive Firms (GKIFs). We have reported on this project already (*People and Performance in Knowledge Intensive Firms: A Comparison of Six Research and Technology Organisations*). This used largely the same employee questionnaire with additional questions on knowledge management. We use data from these questionnaires in Chapter 5 when we look across all of the organisations in the two research projects.

Annexe A to Appendix I:

Case-study organisations – a brief outline

AIT

AIT is a software organisation engaged in the production of information systems solutions for around 20 clients who are mostly in the financial services sector. Established in 1986 by four employees, it has been a plc since 1997, although its status has recently changed and it is now listed on the alternative investment market. At the time of our research it employed around 400 people in Henley-on-Thames, Britain's own 'silicon valley' where the market for experienced, skilled staff is very tight.

The product market is intensely competitive and the technology is changing rapidly. Work is organised around the idea of multiple teams and multiple roles. All employees belong to at least two teams and professional employees belong to three, and this attempts to overcome the normal functional boundary problems found in many larger organisations. Operational teams are based around projects for particular clients and include various specialists under a project manager or director; vocational teams bring together specialists – eg testers or business analysts – and T-groups provide a means of upward and downward communication for all employees.

Our interviews for the employee attitude survey focused on two project teams, and we interviewed 36 non-managerial staff (such as developers, systems analysts and testers) in Year 1 and 33 in Year 2.

(However, as noted earlier, since the period of our research AIT have undergone a number of substantial changes, although the basis of the policies and procedures described here are still in place.)

Clerical Medical

Clerical Medical employs around 2,000 staff and is one of the largest financial services providers in the UK, operating mainly through independent financial advisers. De-mutualisation in 1996 was swiftly followed by a merger. With the Halifax Group, and Clerical Medical it is now part of the Halifax Bank of Scotland's Group Financial Services Division.

Our unit of analysis was customer services, where we focused on four departments: new business services, corporate and executive pensions, final salary, and annuities. During the course of our research a lot of emphasis was placed on improving customer services through a number of HR initiatives, including 'Living the Brand', a campaign aimed at linking individual jobs with the direction of the organisation and improved customer service, and changes at team leader and management level. For our attitude survey we interviewed 29 people in Year 1 and 34 in Year 2, the majority of whom were senior administrators and administrators.

Contact 24

Contact 24 is a call and contact centre based in Bristol which, since September 2000, has been owned by Havas, a large advertising and communication organisation based in France. Contact 24 provides contact and call centre services to a wide range of clients including supermarkets, car manufacturers and financial services organisations. It employs around 950 employees (excluding temporary employees) on two sites, and also provides a managed service activity on two other sites for outside clients.

Contact 24 provides its clients with a variety of services. Dedicated contracts have been increasing recently and involve teams of customer service representatives (CSRs) working exclusively for one client. With the exception of the small bureau which carries out tactical work for a range of clients, the call centres are organised into client teams, ranging from 20 to 200 employees. The organisation works closely with many clients to ensure that the CSRs who work on dedicated project teams are those most suitable for the particular service or product offered. Customer demand varies in often unpredictable ways, creating pressure on managing appropriate staffing levels.

Our employee interviews focused on CSRs from one call centre site, working for four client teams, where we interviewed 33 in Year 1 and 40 in Year 2. The majority of these employees were young (55 per cent were under 30 years of age) and had very short job tenure (only 25 per cent, for example, had worked for the organisation for two years or more) – a fairly typical profile for a call centre workforce.

Jaguar Cars

Jaguar Cars have seen a revival in growth in recent years, resulting in the launch of new models and substantial expansion of manufacturing capacity. Much of this was down to the success of a number of quality initiatives launched in the 1990s, many of which were driven by Ford who took over the organisation in 1989. Today Jaguar has three sites: Browns Lane, Coventry; Castle Bromwich; and the new, revitalised old Ford plant at Halewood.

Our research was conducted at the Browns Lane plant in Coventry. We interviewed 41 manual workers in the first year, mainly from the trim and assembly area, and 37 in the second year.

Nationwide Building Society

Employing around 14,000 staff, Nationwide is the country's largest building society, providing more than 10 million members with a broad range of financial products and services including mortgages, savings, current accounts, life assurance, personal loans and household insurance. In recent years Nationwide has become well known for its commitment to mutuality, and as more and more building societies convert to plc status this characteristic of ownership has come to distinguish it in the marketplace and has been used to its competitive advantage.

The unit of analysis chosen for our study was the sales force for the southern region, which at the time of our first interviews in July 2000 employed 46 financial consultations (FCs), 44 of whom were interviewed on a structured basis for the employee attitude survey in Year 1. By the time of our second survey the sales force had grown, and 49 were interviewed in Year 2. The sales force covers a large geographical area encompassing a wide variety of customer needs. Labour turnover for financial consultants was about 5 per cent, much lower than the industry average, and in our sample just under half (41 per cent) had worked for Nationwide for 10 years or more.

Oxford Magnet Technology

Oxford Magnet Technology (OMT) designs and manufacturers superconducting magnets and is a jointly-owned subsidiary of Siemens and Oxford Instruments. Siemens owns a controlling interest in the firm, but allows complete discretion in operation. This is important to the market position of OMT. Approximately two-thirds of the business conduced by OMT is for Siemens, but the remaining one-third is for a range of other clients.

OMT makes superconducting magnets for use in magnetic resonance imaging (MRI scanning) equipment. The production process is quite involved, and can take as long as 28 days to complete, depending on the magnet being produced. Unfortunately, it is largely impossible to test a magnet during this production process, and so there is a substantial investment in work in progress by the time a magnet reaches the test phase.

Our unit of analysis in OMT consisted of staff surrounding two magnet projects. The attitude survey covered 40 members of the magnet design teams as well as those involved in the assembly of these two products in both Years 1 and 2.

PriceWaterhouse Coopers (PWC)

At the time of our first interviews PriceWaterhouse Coopers (PWC) was still readjusting from the merger between Price Waterhouse and Coopers, which took place in July 1998. Our research focused on one of the five lines of services known as ABAS (Assurance and Business Advisory Services) the main business activity of which is to conduct audits and provide clients with assurance for their business. We looked at three offices in the southern region of ABAS – Southampton, Reading, and Uxbridge, interviewing senior associates, assistant managers and managers for the employee attitude survey. In Year 1 we interviewed 43 employees, but in Year 2 this fell to 27 due to a reorganisation of the ABAS line of business which affected the offices we were studying and made it difficult for us to make realistic comparisons between the two years.

Royal Mint

At the time of our research, the Royal Mint employed around 1,000 staff in the manufacture of circulation coins, collector coinages, coin blanks and medals for both UK and overseas customers. Although it had had market dominance for much of its working life, during the latter half of the 1990s the trading environment began to change, with increased overseas competition, higher customer demands and the threat of the loss of some traditional overseas markets. At the same time, however, the introduction of the single European currency afforded new market opportunities in the form of the Euro and the potential for considerable growth. As a result, major investment took place in capital equipment and new working practices were introduced with an emphasis on quality, flexibility and teamworking.

The unit of analysis was one of the production departments known as MRB (melting, rolling and blanking) where the first stage of the coining process takes place. The workforce here comprises long-serving employees (81 per cent had worked for the Mint for 10 years or more), and was heavily unionised (91 per cent were members of a union). Employees in this area had been top earners in the Mint over the previous 25 years, and had one of the worst employee relations records in the organisation. We interviewed 42 operatives in Year 1 and 33 in Year 2. (Unfortunately, major changes were taking place during the time of the second-year interviews which prevented us from conducting the full number of interviews.)

Royal United Hospital (RUH), Bath

The RUH is a district general hospital employing around 3,500 staff on a single site in Bath. It was a first-wave Trust, achieving trust status in 1992. Like many NHS hospitals, it has been through turbulent times. Five years ago it suffered a financial crisis and brought in a new chief executive who introduced radical changes leading to national recognition and increased funding. However, during the course of our research the Trust suffered further difficulties because of problems with meeting performance targets, changes in the top management team and bad news reported almost daily in local newspapers.

Our research focused on one clinical department where we interviewed 40 staff in the first year and 39 in the second year for our attitude survey. This covered a range of non-managerial jobs both on and off the wards, including nurses, HCAs, administrative staff, technicians and porters.

Selfridges Plc

The Selfridges story is one of corporate renewal where people management has played a vital role in creating a highly successful and expanding, up-market retail department store. Widely described as the embodiment of 'Grace Brothers' in the 1980s and early 1990s, it began the process of renewal and growth in the mid-1990s with the appointment of new management, especially the visionary chief executive, Vittorio Radice. In 1998 Selfridges de-merged from the Sears Group and opened up a new UK store at Trafford Park, Manchester. Subsequently, in 2002 a second store has been opened in Manchester City centre and the Birmingham store will open in 2003.

Selfridges trades as the 'House of brands', and as a consequence a high proportion of sales associates are concessionary staff – in other words, staff not employed by Selfridges at all but by the brand organisation with a concession to sell their products in store. At Trafford Park, for example, some 200 of 450 staff are concessionary staff. To the customer, however, these staff appear to be Selfridges' own staff. In addition there is a heavy reliance on part-time staff (65 per cent at Trafford Centre). These characteristics obviously present challenges in terms of managing the workforce.

The unit of analysis was the Manchester store at Trafford Park, and we focused on two departments – ladies' wear and household. We interviewed 40 sales associates in Year 1 and 41 in Year 2. Of these 95 per cent were women and half were under 30 years of age. Because the store had been open for only a few years the length of service was usually less than two years.

Siemens Medical Solutions

Siemens Medical Solutions is a wholly-owned subsidiary of Siemens AG. It is a market leader, employing 550 staff in the UK, and provides a wide range of high-technology medical capital equipment, IT solutions and managed technology services for the NHS and private health care sector. The division of the organisation we focused on was Technical Customer Services, which deals with the installation, commission and service of all medical equipment made by Siemens, including MRI body scanners incorporating magnets from OMT.

Our employee attitude survey centred on one of five regions – the South-West and Wales region –

and comprised regional service engineers as well as the engineers engaged in the provision of UK technical support and customer service representatives. The technical support team and national call centre staff are based at the UK headquarters for Siemens in Bracknell, while regional service engineers are home-based but are co-ordinated and despatched by the UK call centre. In total 27 employees were interviewed in Year 1 only.

Tesco

Tesco, the largest supermarket chain in the UK, employed (in 1999/2000) around 170,000 staff in 659 stores across the country. The organisation underwent considerable change in the mid-1990s in order to improve its competitive position, with a much greater emphasis on a customer-facing culture. Through a policy of improving customer service and lowering prices Tesco has successfully increased its market share in recent years, although the industry has seen very little growth.

One of the characteristics of Tesco which particularly attracted us to this organisation for research purposes was the operation of highly standardised policies, procedures and processes across all stores, including HR policies. Our research focused on four stores in a single region. All were in market towns with similar socio-economic profiles. Our interviews for the employee attitude survey were with the section manager population (a first line manager's position). In Year 1 we interviewed 43 section managers, representing two-thirds of the section manager population in those stores, and in Year 2 we interviewed 40 section managers.

Appendix 2:

Tables showing changes in employee attitudes in selected organisations

Figures based on mean scores

Table 18 | Changes in selected employee attitudes: the RUH, Year 1 to Year 2
Mean scores (based on 5-point scale)

	Year 1	Year 2
HR policy practices		
Job influence	3.00	3.11
Appraisal	3.06	3.97
Sense of teamworking	4.18	4.35
Work–life balance	2.10	2.30
Management		
Leadership – respond to suggestions	2.74	3.03
Leadership – dealing with problems	2.85	3.33
Respect shown by the line manager	3.73	4.32
Outcomes		
Job satisfaction	3.83	4.09
Motivation (4-point scale)	2.85	3.27
Commitment (sharing the values)	2.85	3.38
n =	42	39

Table 19 | Changes in selected staff attitudes: Selfridges, Year 1 to Year 2
Mean scores (5-point scale)

	Year 1	Year 2
Appraisal satisfaction	3.53	4.03
Manager good at responding to suggestions	3.15	3.45
Respect shown by immediate line manager	4.20	4.56
Job influence	3.10	3.66
Job satisfaction	3.75	4.22
Motivation (4-point scale)	3.18	3.39
Commitment/loyalty to Selfridges	4.08	4.12
n =	40	41

Table 20 | Changes in selected staff attitudes: Nationwide, Year 1 to Year 2
Mean scores (5-point scale)

	Year 1	Year 2
Job security	4.21	3.86
Job influence	4.02	3.86
Job satisfaction	4.20	4.06
Motivation (4-point scale)	3.34	3.39
Pay	4.27	4.14
Managers good at responding to suggestions	3.82	3.81
Managers good at dealing with problems at workplace	3.88	3.78
Respect shown the line manager	4.27	4.31
Commitment – pride	4.39	4.29
– loyalty	4.39	4.37
– sharing the values	4.41 (87%)	4.43 (98%)
	n = 44	49

References

APPELBAUM, E., BAILEY, T. and BERG, P. (2000)

Manufacturing Advantage: Why high- performance systems pay off. London, Economic Policy Institute: Cornell University Press.

ARTHUR, J. B. (1992)

'The link between business strategy and industrial relations systems in American steel minimills', *Industrial and Labor Relations Review*, Vol. 45:3, April, p488–506.

ARTHUR, J. B. (1994)

'Effects of human resource systems on manufacturing performance and turnover', *Academy of Management Journal*, Vol. 37:3, p670–687.

BARTEL, A. (2000)

Human Resource Management and Performance in the Service Sector: The case of bank branches. NBER Working Paper Series. Cambridge, MA: National Bureau of Economic Research.

BATT, R. and MOYNIHAN, L. (2002)

'The viability of alternative call centre production models', *Human Resource Management Journal*, Vol. 12, No.4.

BERG, P., APPELBAUM, E., BAILEY, T. and KALLEBERG, A. (1996)

'The performance effects of modular production in the apparel industry', *Industrial Relations*, 35(3): 356–373.

BOXALL, P and PURCELL, J. (2003)

Strategy and Human Resource Management. London: Palgrave.

COYLE-SHAPIRO, J. and KESSLER, I. (2000)

'Consequences of the psychological contract for the employment relationship: a large-scale survey', *Journal of Management Studies*, 37(7): 903–930.

COYLE-SHAPIRO, S., KESSLER, I and PURCELL, S.

'Exploring organizationally directed citizenship behaviour; reciprocity or"its my job",' *Journal of Management Studies.*

FOX, A. (1974)

Beyond Contract: Work, power and trust relations. London: Faber.

GOYDER (1998)

Living Tomorrow's Company. Aldershot, Gower.

GUEST, P., KING, Z. and CONWAY, N. (2001)

Voices from the Boardroom. London: CIPD.

HUTCHINSON, S., KINNIE, N., PURCELL, J., COLLINSON, M., SCARBOROUGH, H. and TERRY, M. (1998)

Getting Fit, Staying Fit: Developing lean and responsive ways of working. London: IPD.

HUSELID, M. (1995)

'The impact of human resource management practices on turnover, productivity and corporate financial performance', *Academy of Management Journal*, Vol. 38, No.3, pp635–672.

KAPLAN, R. and NORTON, D. (1996)

The Balanced Scorecard: Translating strategy into action. Harvard Business School Press.

KING, Z. (2003)

'New or traditional careers? A study of UK graduates' preferences', *Human Resource Management Journal*, Vol. 13, No.1.

MARCHINGTON, M. (2001)

'Employee Involvement at work', in J. Storey (ed.), *Human Resource Management: A critical text.* 2nd edition. London: Thomson.

RUCCI, A., KIRN, S. and QUINN R. (1998)

'The employee – customer – profit chain at Sears', *Harvard Business Review*, Vol. 76, No 1, pp82–97

PFEFFER, J. (1994)

Competitive Advantage through People. Boston: Harvard Business School Press.

PFEFFER, J. (1998)

The Human Equation: Building profits by putting people first. Boston: Harvard Business School Press.

SWART, J., KINNIE, N. and PURCELL, J. (2003)

People and Performance in Knowledge Intensive Firms. London: CIPD.

THOMPSON, M. (2000)

Final Report: The bottom line benefits of strategic human resource management. The UK Aerospace People Management Audit. The Society of British Aerospace Companies.

WEST, M. A., BORRILL C. S., DAWSON, C., SCULLY, J., CARTER, M., ANELAY, S., PATTERSON, M. and WARING, J. (2002)

'The link between the management of employees and patient mortality in acute hospitals', *International Journal of Human Resource Management*, 13: 8 December, 1299–1310.

WRIGHT, P. and SNELL, S. (1998)

'Toward a unifying framework for exploring fit and flexibility in strategic human resource management', *Academy of Management Review*, 23(4): 756–772.

WRIGHT, P. M. and GARDNER, T. M. (2000)

Theoretical and Empirical Challenges in Studying the HR Practice – Firm Performance Relationship. Paper for the European Institute for Advanced Studies in Management.

WRIGHT, P. M., GARDNER, T. M. and TIMOTHY, M. (2003)

'The impact of human resource practices on Business unit operating and financial performance', *Human Resource Management Journal*, Vol 13, No. 10.